New Anti-Inflammatory Diet Cookbook for Beginners 2023

1600

Days Vibrant & Fresh Recipes Heal your Body Naturally and Eating Well | 6-Week Meal Plan for No More Inflammation

Judith M. Tomita

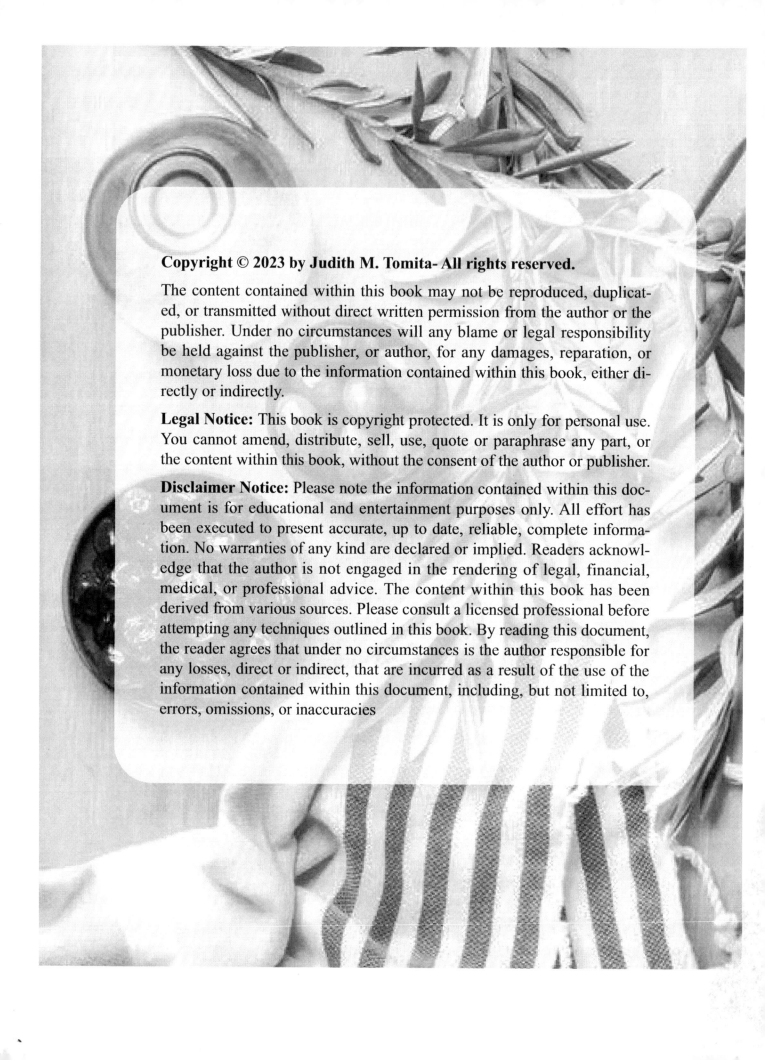

CONTENTS

INTRODUCTION I

Anti-inflammatory Diet? II
How can an anti-inflammatory diet harmonise your health? II
Menus and taboos in the Anti-inflammatory Diet III
Who needs an Anti-inflammatory Diet? IV

6-Week Meal Plan V

Measurement Conversions VIII

Breakfast And Brunch 5

Broccoli Hash Browns 5
Breakfast Bake Millet With Blueberry 5
Mango Rice Pudding...6
Almond Flour English Muffins 6
Strawberry & Pecan Breakfast 6
Green Veggie Frittata 7
Orange-carrot Muffins With Cherries 7
Breakfast Vanilla Quinoa Bowl..8
Tofu Scramble 8
Morning Matcha & Ginger Shake...8
Omelette With Smoky Shrimp 9
Blueberry Smoothie With Ginger 9
Choco-berry Smoothie...10
Almond & Raisin Granola 10
Carrot-strawberry Smoothie..10
No-bread Avocado Sandwich 11

Sauces, Condiments, And Dressings 12

Creamy Dressing With Sesame..12
Old Fashioned Dressing With Lemon And Mustard.......................................12
Fragrant Peach Butter 13
Garlicky Sauce With Tahini 13
Commercial And Mild Curry Powder 14
Caramelized Roasted Fennel With Sunflower Seed Pesto 14
Dairy Free Apple Cider Vinegar With Tangy Barbecue Sauce 15
Delicious Pesto With Kale 15
To Die For Homemade Mayonnaise 16
Traditional And Delightful Gremolata Sauce 16
Game Changer Pickled Red Onions 16

Decadent And Simple Alfredo With Cauliflower 17
Satisfying And Thick Dressing With Avocado 17
Tricky Cheesy Yellow Sauce 17
Fresh Maple Dressing 18
Natural Dressing With Ginger And Turmeric 18

Salads 19

Arugula Salad With Salmon 19
Spinach & Pomegranate Salad 19
Fragrant Coconut Fruit Salad 20
Summer Time Sizzling Green Salad With Salmon 20
Minty Eggplant Salad 21
Convenient Salad With Raspberry Vinaigrette, Spinach, And Walnut 21
Mango Rice Salad With Lime Dressing 21
Carrot Salad With Cherries & Pecans 22
All Green Salad With Basil-cherry Dressing 22
Cucumber & Pear Rice Salad 22
Out Of This World Salad With Basil And Tomato 23
Superb Salad With Chickpea 23
Spinach Salad With Cranberries 23
Summer Salad 24
African Zucchini Salad 24
Nutritious Bowl With Lentil, Vegetable, And Fruit 25

Vegetarian Mains 26

Habanero Pinto Bean & Bell Pepper Pot 26
Homemade Burgers With Bean And Yam 26
Appetizing Casserole With Broccoli And Bean 27
Teriyaki Vegetable Stir-fry 27
Pressure Cooked Ratatouille 27
Soft Zucchini With White Beans And Olives Stuffing 28
Favourite Pizza With Quinoa Flatbread 28
Traditional Cilantro Pilaf 29
Vegetable & Hummus Pizza 29
Chinese Fried Rice 30
Peanuty Sugar Snaps With Lime And Satay Tofu 30
Watercress & Mushroom Spaghetti 31
Seitan Cauliflower Gratin 31
Magical One-pot Tomato Basil Pasta 32
Spicy And Tasty Indian Cauliflower And Broccoli Rabe 32
Cheesy Cauliflower Casserole 33

Soups & Stews 34

One-pot Chunky Beef Stew 34
Native Asian Soup With Squash And Shitake 34

Winterrific Soup With Chicken And Dumpling 35
Chicken & Ginger Soup 35
Rosemary White Bean Soup 36
Soulful Roasted Vegetable Soup 36
Cold Vegetable Soup 37
Rice Noodle Soup With Beans 37
Green Bean & Zucchini Velouté 37
Turmeric Cauliflower Soup 38
Green Bean & Rice Soup 38
Cayenne Pumpkin Soup 39
Brussels Sprouts & Tofu Soup 39
Vegetable Chili 40
Power Green Soup 40
Mediterranean Stew With Lentil And Broccoli 41

Poultry And Meats 42

Chicken Stir-fry With Bell Pepper 42
Magnificent Herbaceous Pork Meatballs 42
Lemon & Caper Turkey Scaloppine 43
Herby Green Whole Chicken 43
Apple-glazed Whole Chicken 44
Italian Turkey Meatballs 44
Appetizing And Healthy Turkey Gumbo 45
Gingered Beef Stir-fry With Peppers 45
Nut Free Turkey Burgers With Ginger 46
Traditional Beef Bolognese 46
Cumin Lamb Meatballs With Aioli 47
Veggie & Beef Brisket 47
Tastylicious Chicken Cajun With Prawn 48
Homemade Chicken & Pepper Cacciatore 48
Sweet Balsamic Chicken 49
Korean Vegetable Salad With Smoky Crispy Kalua Pork 49

Fish And Seafood 50

Hawaiian Tuna 50
Wonderful Baked Sea Bass With Tomatoes, Olives, And Capers 50
Grilled Adobo Shrimp Skewers 51
Crispy Pan-seared Salmon 51
Tasty Sardine Donburi 52
Hazelnut Crusted Trout Fillets 52
Appealing Lemon With Wild Salmon And Mixed Vegetables 53
Spicy Shrimp Scampi 53
Old Bay Crab Cakes 54
Lime Salmon Burgers 54
Smoky Boneless Haddock With Pea Risotto 55
Nostalgic Tuna And Avocado Salad Sandwiches 55

Salmon In Miso-ginger Sauce 56
Dazzling And Smoky Salmon Hash Browns 56
Creamy Crabmeat 57
Greatest Crispy Fish Tacos And Mango Salsa 57

Smoothies 58

Savoury Smoothie With Mango And Thyme 58
Minty Juice With Pineapple And Cucumber 58
Handy Veggie Smoothie 58
Cheery Cherry Smoothie 59
For Advanced Green Juice 59
Salad-like Green Smoothie 59
Refreshing Green Iced Tea With Ginger 60
Great Watermelon Smoothie 60
Smoothie That Can Soothe Inflammation 60
Fabolous Minty Green Smoothie 61
Pain Reliever Smoothie 61
Tropical And Extra Red Smoothie 61
Mediterranean Green On Green Smoothie 62
Fantastic Fruity Smoothie 62
Wild Blueberry Smoothie With Chocolate And Turmeric 62
Popular Banana Smoothie With Kale 63

Desserts 64

Peanut Chocolate Brownies 64
Mini Chocolate Fudge Squares 64
Tasty Haystack Cookies From Missouri 65
Coconut & Chocolate Cake 65
Spiced Supreme Orange 66
Mango & Coconut Rice Pudding 66
Chocolate Campanelle With Hazelnuts 66
Lemon Blackberry Cake 67
Vanilla Berry Tarts 67
Poached Pears With Green Tea 68
Tropical Cheesecake 68
Full Coconut Cake 68
Nutty Date Cake 69
Mango Chocolate Fudge 69
Coconut & Chocolate Brownies 70
Vanilla Brownies 70

Appendix:Recipes Index 71

INTRODUCTION

Judith M. Tomita, a celebrated nutritionist, culinary artist, and advocate for holistic wellness, takes you on an enlightening culinary journey. Drawing on her extensive research and personal experience in combating inflammation through food, she has crafted a collection of recipes designed not only to tantalize your taste buds but to heal, rejuvenate, and energize your body.

This book is not just a cookbook; it's a lifestyle guide. It showcases a wide array of whole, nutrient-rich foods that form the basis of the anti-inflammatory diet. From luscious fruits and vibrant vegetables to lean proteins, whole grains, and heart-healthy fats, Tomita encourages readers to embrace foods that nurture the body. She guides you away from processed, refined, and pro-inflammatory ingredients, offering alternatives that are just as delicious and satisfying.

Each recipe in this cookbook is a testament to Tomita's culinary creativity and her commitment to making healthy eating a joyous experience. Whether you're a seasoned chef or a kitchen novice, her detailed instructions, insightful tips, and mouth-watering photographs will inspire confidence and curiosity. From breakfast delights and nourishing soups to elegant main courses and delectable desserts, every dish is crafted with care, love, and a deep understanding of the ingredients' healing properties.

Judith M. Tomita's Anti-Inflammatory Diet Cookbook is more than a collection of recipes; it's a beacon of hope for those seeking a path to health through the pleasure of eating. It invites you to embark on a culinary adventure that recognizes food not as mere sustenance but as medicine, art, and celebration. Here's to a journey of healing, vitality, and joy, all served on a platter of wisdom and creativity.

Anti-inflammatory Diet?

The anti-inflammatory diet is an eating pattern designed to reduce chronic inflammation in the body, which has been linked to various health issues. It emphasizes the consumption of whole, nutrient-rich foods such as fruits, vegetables, whole grains, lean proteins, healthy fats like omega-3 fatty acids, and spices known for their anti-inflammatory properties, such as turmeric and ginger. At the same time, it advises limiting or avoiding processed foods, red meats, refined sugars, and excessive alcohol, all of which may contribute to inflammation. By promoting a balanced and mindful approach to eating, the anti-inflammatory diet aims to support overall health and well-being, potentially alleviating symptoms of chronic inflammatory conditions and supporting heart and gut health.

How can an anti-inflammatory diet harmonise your health?

Reduces Chronic Inflammation

By focusing on foods that combat inflammation, this diet can help alleviate chronic inflammatory conditions such as rheumatoid arthritis, inflammatory bowel disease, and more.

Supports Heart Health

Including healthy fats and whole grains while avoiding processed foods can improve cholesterol levels and blood pressure, reducing the risk of heart disease.

Aids in Weight Management

The diet emphasizes nutrient-dense, satisfying foods that can help control hunger and assist in weight loss or maintenance.

Enhances Gut Health

By promoting foods that foster a healthy gut microbiome, the diet may improve digestion and boost the immune system.

Improves Mental Health

Some research suggests that reducing inflammation may have a positive impact on mental health, including reducing symptoms of depression and anxiety.

Boosts Skin Health

Anti-inflammatory foods rich in antioxidants may contribute to clearer, healthier skin.

Promotes Overall Wellness

By encouraging a balanced and mindful approach to eating, the diet can contribute to improved overall health, increased energy levels, and a sense of well-being.

Customizable to Individual Needs

The principles of the anti-inflammatory diet can be adapted to suit individual preferences, allergies, or intolerances, making it accessible to many.

Menus and taboos in the Anti-inflammatory Diet

Can Eat (Anti-Inflammatory Foods):

 1. Fruits & Vegetables: Preferably colorful and varied, like berries, cherries, spinach, kale, and broccoli.

 2. Whole Grains: Such as brown rice, quinoa, whole wheat, and oats.

 3. Healthy Fats: Including olive oil, avocados, and fatty fish (salmon, mackerel, sardines) rich in omega-3 fatty acids.

 4. Lean Proteins: Poultry, fish, beans, lentils, and tofu.

 5. Nuts & Seeds: Such as almonds, walnuts, chia seeds, and flaxseeds.

 6. Herbs & Spices: Including turmeric, ginger, garlic, cinnamon, and rosemary.

 7. Green Tea: Rich in antioxidants.

 8. Water & Herbal Teas: For proper hydration.

Should Avoid(Pro-Inflammatory Foods):

1. Processed Foods: Including packaged snacks, fast food, and canned goods with added preservatives.

2. Red and Processed Meats: Such as bacon, sausages, and hot dogs.

3. Refined Sugars & Carbohydrates: Found in white bread, pastries, candies, and sodas.

4. Trans Fats & Unhealthy Oils: Often found in margarine, fried foods, and some packaged products.

5. Excessive Alcohol: Limit alcohol consumption or choose red wine in moderation.

6. Dairy Products: Some individuals may need to limit or avoid dairy, depending on personal sensitivities.

7. Certain Cooking Methods: Avoid frying or charbroiling, which may create harmful compounds.

Who needs an Anti-inflammatory Diet?

Individuals with Chronic Inflammatory Conditions: Chronic inflammatory diseases such as rheumatoid arthritis, lupus, and inflammatory bowel diseases are marked by persistent inflammation in the body. This inflammation often leads to pain, swelling, and sometimes irreversible damage to affected tissues. Adopting an anti-inflammatory diet can reduce the intake of inflammation-promoting foods, thereby potentially lessening symptoms, slowing disease progression, and improving quality of life.

People with Heart Disease or Risk Factors: Heart disease is often linked to inflammation within the blood vessels and heart. Individuals with high cholesterol, hypertension, or those at risk due to genetic factors could greatly benefit from an anti-inflammatory diet. By emphasizing heart-healthy fats, whole grains, and antioxidants, the diet may reduce inflammation, improve blood flow, and decrease the risk of heart attacks and strokes.

Individuals Struggling with Weight Management: Obesity is itself a pro-inflammatory state, contributing to chronic systemic inflammation. An anti-inflammatory diet, rich in fiber, healthy fats, and lean proteins, promotes a balanced way of eating. This can lead to weight loss or help in maintaining a healthy weight, further reducing the levels of inflammation in the body and improving overall well-being.

People with Type 2 Diabetes: Type 2 diabetes often results in chronic inflammation, exacerbating insulin resistance. An anti-inflammatory diet focuses on balanced food choices that help regulate blood sugar and improve insulin sensitivity. This diet can thus play a significant role in managing type 2 diabetes, making it a valuable tool in a comprehensive diabetes care plan.

Individuals with Skin Conditions: Skin conditions like acne, eczema, or rosacea are often linked to underlying inflammation. An anti-inflammatory diet that excludes potential allergens and includes nutrient-rich foods can promote healthier skin, reduce flare-ups, and assist in the healing process, offering a complementary approach to traditional treatments.

People with Mental Health Conditions: Emerging research shows a connection between mental health conditions such as depression and anxiety and inflammation in the body. An anti-inflammatory diet may support mental health by reducing inflammation, thereby potentially alleviating symptoms and improving mood and cognitive function.

Individuals with Autoimmune Disorders: Autoimmune disorders like Hashimoto's thyroiditis and multiple sclerosis occur when the immune system mistakenly attacks the body's tissues. An anti-inflammatory diet can mitigate this overactive immune response, possibly offering symptom relief and improving daily functioning.

6-Week Meal Plan

Day	Breakfast	Lunch	Dinner
1	Broccoli Hash Browns 5	Chicken Stir-fry With Bell Pepper 42	Cold Vegetable Soup 37
2	Breakfast Bake Millet With Blueberry 5	Magnificent Herbaceous Pork Meatballs 42	Rice Noodle Soup With Beans 37
3	Mango Rice Pudding 6	Lemon & Caper Turkey Scaloppine 43	Green Bean & Zucchini Velouté 37
4	Almond Flour English Muffins 6	Herby Green Whole Chicken 43	Turmeric Cauliflower Soup 38
5	Strawberry & Pecan Breakfast 6	Apple-glazed Whole Chicken 44	Mediterranean Stew With Lentil And Broccoli 41
6	Green Veggie Frittata 7	Italian Turkey Meatballs 44	Cayenne Pumpkin Soup 39
7	Orange-carrot Muffins With Cherries 7	Appetizing And Healthy Turkey Gumbo 45	Brussels Sprouts & Tofu Soup 39
8	Breakfast Vanilla Quinoa Bowl 8	Gingered Beef Stir-fry With Peppers 45	Coconut & Chocolate Brownies 70
9	Tofu Scramble 8	Nut Free Turkey Burgers With Ginger 46	Poached Pears With Green Tea 68
10	Morning Matcha & Ginger Shake 8	Traditional Beef Bolognese 46	Tropical Cheesecake 68
11	Omelette With Smoky Shrimp 9	Cumin Lamb Meatballs With Aioli 47	Full Coconut Cake 68
12	Blueberry Smoothie With Ginger 9	Veggie & Beef Brisket 47	Nutty Date Cake 69
13	Choco-berry Smoothie 10	Tastylicious Chicken Cajun With Prawn 48	Mango Chocolate Fudge 69
14	Almond & Raisin Granola 10	Homemade Chicken & Pepper Cacciatore 48	Vanilla Brownies 70

Day	Breakfast	Lunch	Dinner
15	Carrot-strawberry Smoothie 10	Sweet Balsamic Chicken 49	Power Green Soup 40
16	No-bread Avocado Sandwich 11	Korean Vegetable Salad With Smoky Crispy Kalua Pork 49	Green Bean & Rice Soup 38
17	Arugula Salad With Salmon 19	Hawaiian Tuna 50	Savoury Smoothie With Mango And Thyme 58
18	Spinach & Pomegranate Salad 19	Grilled Adobo Shrimp Skewers 51	Minty Juice With Pineapple And Cucumber 58
19	Fragrant Coconut Fruit Salad 20	Wonderful Baked Sea Bass With Tomatoes, Olives, And Capers 50	Handy Veggie Smoothie 58
20	Summer Time Sizzling Green Salad With Salmon 20	Crispy Pan-seared Salmon 51	Cheery Cherry Smoothie 59
21	Minty Eggplant Salad 21	Tasty Sardine Donburi 52	For Advanced Green Juice 59
22	Mango Rice Salad With Lime Dressing 21	Hazelnut Crusted Trout Fillets 52	Salad-like Green Smoothie 59
23	Convenient Salad With Raspberry Vinaigrette, Spinach, And Walnut 21	Appealing Lemon With Wild Salmon And Mixed Vegetables 53	Refreshing Green Iced Tea With Ginger 60
24	Carrot Salad With Cherries & Pecans 22	Spicy Shrimp Scampi 53	Great Watermelon Smoothie 60
25	All Green Salad With Basil-cherry Dressing 22	Old Bay Crab Cakes 54	Smoothie That Can Soothe Inflammation 60
26	Cucumber & Pear Rice Salad 22	Lime Salmon Burgers 54	Fabolous Minty Green Smoothie 61
27	Out Of This World Salad With Basil And Tomato 23	Smoky Boneless Haddock With Pea Risotto 55	Pain Reliever Smoothie 61
28	Seitan Cauliflower Gratin 31	Magical One-pot Tomato Basil Pasta 32	Tropical And Extra Red Smoothie 61

Day	Breakfast	Lunch	Dinner
29	Superb Salad With Chickpea 23	Nostalgic Tuna And Avocado Salad Sandwiches 55	Mediterranean Green On Green Smoothie 62
30	Spinach Salad With Cranberries 23	Salmon In Miso-ginger Sauce 56	Fantastic Fruity Smoothie 62
31	Summer Salad 24	Dazzling And Smoky Salmon Hash Browns 56	Wild Blueberry Smoothie With Chocolate And Turmeric 62
32	African Zucchini Salad 24	Creamy Crabmeat 57	Popular Banana Smoothie With Kale 63
33	African Zucchini Salad 25	Greatest Crispy Fish Tacos And Mango Salsa 57	Peanut Chocolate Brownies 64
34	Habanero Pinto Bean & Bell Pepper Pot 26	Spicy And Tasty Indian Cauliflower And Broccoli Rabe 32	Mini Chocolate Fudge Squares 64
35	Homemade Burgers With Bean And Yam 26	Cheesy Cauliflower Casserole 33	Tasty Haystack Cookies From Missouri 65
36	Appetizing Casserole With Broccoli And Bean 27	One-pot Chunky Beef Stew 34	Coconut & Chocolate Cake 65
37	Teriyaki Vegetable Stir-fry 27	Native Asian Soup With Squash And Shitake 34	Spiced Supreme Orange 66
38	Pressure Cooked Ratatouille 27	Winterrific Soup With Chicken And Dumpling 35	Mango & Coconut Rice Pudding 66
39	Favourite Pizza With Quinoa Flatbread 28	Chicken & Ginger Soup 35	Chocolate Campanelle With Hazelnuts 66
40	Traditional Cilantro Pilaf 29	Rosemary White Bean Soup 36	Lemon Blackberry Cake 67
41	Chinese Fried Rice 30	Soulful Roasted Vegetable Soup 36	Vanilla Berry Tarts 67
42	Watercress & Mushroom Spaghetti 31	Vegetable Chili 40	Poached Pears With Green Tea 68

Measurement Conversions

BASIC KITCHEN CONVERSIONS & EQUIVALENTS

DRY MEASUREMENTS CONVERSION CHART

3 TEASPOONS = 1 TABLESPOON = 1/16 CUP

6 TEASPOONS = 2 TABLESPOONS = 1/8 CUP

12 TEASPOONS = 4 TABLESPOONS = 1/4 CUP

24 TEASPOONS = 8 TABLESPOONS = 1/2 CUP

36 TEASPOONS = 12 TABLESPOONS = 3/4 CUP

48 TEASPOONS = 16 TABLESPOONS = 1 CUP

METRIC TO US COOKING CONVERSIONS

OVEN TEMPERATURES

120 °C = 250 °F

160 °C = 320 °F

180° C = 350 °F

205 °C = 400 °F

220 °C = 425 °F

LIQUID MEASUREMENTS CONVERSION CHART

8 FLUID OUNCES = 1 CUP = 1/2 PINT = 1/4 QUART

16 FLUID OUNCES = 2 CUPS = 1 PINT = 1/2 QUART

32 FLUID OUNCES = 4 CUPS = 2 PINTS = 1 QUART= 1/4 GALLON

128 FLUID OUNCES = 16 CUPS = 8 PINTS = 4 QUARTS = 1 GALLON

BAKING IN GRAMS

1 CUP FLOUR = 140 GRAMS

1 CUP SUGAR = 150 GRAMS

1 CUP POWDERED SUGAR = 160 GRAMS

1 CUP HEAVY CREAM = 235 GRAMS

VOLUME

1 MILLILITER = 1/5 TEASPOON

5 ML = 1 TEASPOON

15 ML = 1 TABLESPOON

240 ML = 1 CUP OR 8 FLUID OUNCES

1 LITER = 34 FL. OUNCES

WEIGHT

1 GRAM = .035 OUNCES

100 GRAMS = 3.5 OUNCES

500 GRAMS = 1.1 POUNDS

1 KILOGRAM = 35 OUNCES

US TO METRIC COOKING CONVERSIONS

1/5 TSP = 1 ML

1 TSP = 5 ML

1 TBSP = 15 ML

1 FL OUNCE = 30 ML

1 CUP = 237 ML

1 PINT (2 CUPS) = 473 ML

1 QUART (4 CUPS) = .95 LITER

1 GALLON (16 CUPS) = 3.8 LITERS

1 OZ = 28 GRAMS

1 POUND = 454 GRAMS

BUTTER

1 CUP BUTTER = 2 STICKS = 8 OUNCES = 230 GRAMS = 8 TABLESPOONS

WHAT DOES 1 CUP EQUAL

1 CUP = 8 FLUID OUNCES

1 CUP = 16 TABLESPOONS

1 CUP = 48 TEASPOONS

1 CUP = 1/2 PINT

1 CUP = 1/4 QUART

1 CUP = 1/16 GALLON

1 CUP = 240 ML

BAKING PAN CONVERSIONS

1 CUP ALL-PURPOSE FLOUR = 4.5 OZ

1 CUP ROLLED OATS = 3 OZ 1 LARGE EGG = 1.7OZ

1 CUP BUTTER = 8 OZ 1 CUP MILK = 8 OZ

1 CUP HEAVY CREAM = 8.4 OZ

1 CUP GRANULATED SUGAR = 7.1 OZ

1 CUP PACKED BROWN SUGAR = 7.75 OZ

1 CUP VEGETABLE OIL = 7.7 OZ

1 CUP UNSIFTED POWDERED SUGAR = 4.4 OZ

BAKING PAN CONVERSIONS

9-INCH ROUND CAKE PAN = 12 CUPS

10-INCH TUBE PAN =16 CUPS

11-INCH BUNDT PAN = 12 CUPS

9-INCH SPRINGFORM PAN = 10 CUPS

9 X 5 INCH LOAF PAN = 8 CUPS

9-INCH SQUARE PAN = 8 CUPS

Breakfast And Brunch

Broccoli Hash Browns

Servings: 4
Cooking Time: 35 Minutes

Ingredients:

- 3 eggs
- 1 head broccoli, cut into florets
- ½ white onion, grated
- Sea salt and pepper to taste
- 5 tbsp coconut oil

Directions:

1. Pour the broccoli into a food processor and pulse a few times until smoothly grated. Transfer the broccoli into a bowl, add the eggs, white onion, salt, and black pepper. Use a spoon to mix the ingredients evenly and set aside 5-10 minutes to firm up a bit. Place a large skillet over medium heat and drop 1/3 of the coconut oil to warm.

2. Ladle scoops of the broccoli mixture into the skillet. Flatten the pancakes to measure 3 to 4 inches in diameter, and fry until golden brown on one side, 4 minutes. Turn the pancakes with a spatula and cook for another 5 minutes.

3. Transfer the hash browns to a serving plate and repeat the frying process for the remaining broccoli mixture. Serve the hash browns warm with green salad.

Nutrition Info:

- Per Serving: Calories: 207;Fat: 23g;Protein: 5g;Carbs: 3g.

Breakfast Bake Millet With Blueberry

Servings: 8
Cooking Time: 55 Minutes

Ingredients:

- 2 cups millet, soaked in water overnight
- 2 cups blueberries, fresh or frozen
- 1 ¾ cups applesauce, unsweetened
- ⅓ cup melted coconut oil
- 2 teaspoons ginger, freshly grated
- 1 ½ teaspoons cinnamon, ground

Directions:

1. Preheat the oven to 350° F.
2. For 1 to 2 minutes, drain and rinse the millet in a fine-mesh sieve. Transfer it to a large bowl.
3. Gently fold in the blueberries, applesauce, coconut oil, ginger, and cinnamon.
4. Into a 9-by-9-inch casserole dish, pour the mixture into it. Then cover it with aluminum foil.
5. For 40 minutes, place the dish in the preheated oven and bake. Remove the foil and bake for 10 to 15 minutes more, or until the top is lightly crisp.

Nutrition Info:

- Per Serving: Calories: 323 ;Fat: 13g ;Protein: 6g ;Carbs: 48g .

Mango Rice Pudding

Servings: 4
Cooking Time: 30 Minutes

Ingredients:

- 1 cup brown rice
- 1 ½ cups non-dairy milk
- 3 tbsp pure date sugar
- 2 tsp pumpkin pie spice
- 1 mango, chopped
- 2 tbsp chopped walnuts

Directions:

1. In a pot over medium heat, add the rice, 2 cups water, milk, sugar, and pumpkin pie spice. Bring to a boil, lower the heat and simmer for 18-20 minutes until the rice is soft and the liquid is absorbed. Put in the mango and stir to combine. Top with walnuts. Serve and enjoy!

Nutrition Info:

- Per Serving: Calories: 312;Fat: 4.9g;Protein: 5g;Carbs: 64.6g.

Almond Flour English Muffins

Servings: 4
Cooking Time: 20 Minutes

Ingredients:

- 2 eggs
- 2 tbsp almond flour
- ½ tsp baking powder
- 1 pinch of sea salt
- 3 tbsp peanut butter

Directions:

1. In a bowl, combine the almond flour, baking powder, and salt. Then, pour in the eggs and whisk. Let the batter sit for 5 minutes to set. Melt the peanut butter in a frying pan and add the mixture in four dollops. Fry until golden brown on one side, then flip the bread with a spatula and fry further until golden brown. Serve.

Nutrition Info:

- Per Serving: Calories: 123;Fat: 9.2g;Protein: 6.5g;Carbs: 3.5g.

Strawberry & Pecan Breakfast

Servings: 2
Cooking Time: 15 Minutes

Ingredients:

- 1 can coconut milk, refrigerated overnight
- 1 cup granola
- ½ cup pecans, chopped
- 1 cup sliced strawberries

Directions:

1. Drain the coconut milk liquid. Layer the coconut milk solids, granola, and strawberries in small glasses. Top with chopped pecans and serve right away.

Nutrition Info:

- Per Serving: Calories: 644;Fat: 79g;Protein: 23g;Carbs: 82g.

Green Veggie Frittata

Servings: 4
Cooking Time: 25 Minutes

Ingredients:

- 1 cup mushrooms, sliced
- 8 eggs
- 1 leek, chopped
- 2 tbsp avocado oil
- ½ tsp garlic powder
- ½ tsp dried basil
- 1 cup baby spinach
- Sea salt and pepper to taste

Directions:

1. Preheat your oven to 400°F. Warm the avocado oil in a skillet over medium heat and place the leeks. Sauté for 5 minutes until soft. Beat the eggs, garlic, basil, and salt in a bowl. Pour the egg mixture in the skillet and cook for 5 minutes, stirring often. Stir in mushrooms, spinach, and pepper and bake for 10 minutes. Serve immediately.

Nutrition Info:

- Per Serving: Calories: 280;Fat: 18g;Protein: 18g;Carbs: 156g.

Orange-carrot Muffins With Cherries

Servings: 6
Cooking Time: 45 Minutes

Ingredients:

- 1 tsp avocado oil
- 2 tbsp almond butter
- ¼ cup non-dairy milk
- 1 orange, peeled
- 1 carrot, coarsely chopped
- 2 tbsp chopped dried cherries
- 3 tbsp molasses
- 2 tbsp ground flaxseed
- 1 tsp apple cider vinegar
- 1 tsp pure vanilla extract
- ½ tsp ground cinnamon
- ½ tsp ground ginger
- ¼ tsp ground nutmeg
- ¼ tsp allspice
- ¾ cup whole-wheat flour
- 1 tsp baking powder
- ½ tsp baking soda
- ½ cup rolled oats
- 2 tbsp raisins
- 2 tbsp sunflower seeds

Directions:

1. Preheat your oven to 350°F. Grease 6 muffin cups with avocado oil. In a food processor, add the almond butter, milk, orange, carrot, cherries, molasses, flaxseed, vinegar, vanilla, cinnamon, ginger, nutmeg, and allspice and blend until smooth. In a bowl, combine the flour, baking powder, and baking soda. Fold in the wet mixture and gently stir to combine. Mix in the oats, raisins, and sunflower seeds. Divide the batter between muffin cups. Put in a baking tray and bake for 30 minutes.

Nutrition Info:

- Per Serving: Calories: 210;Fat: 5g;Protein: 5.3g;Carbs: 36.6g.

Breakfast Vanilla Quinoa Bowl

Servings: 4
Cooking Time: 15 Minutes

Ingredients:

- 1 cup quinoa
- 2 tbsp maple syrup
- 1 tsp vanilla extract
- 1 ½ cups water
- A pinch of sea salt

Directions:

1. Place all the ingredients into your Instant Pot. Stir to combine well. Seal the lid and cook on "Manual" on High for 1 minute. Once ready, perform a quick pressure release by turning the valve to "venting". Carefully open the lid, fluff with a fork and serve warm. Enjoy!

Nutrition Info:

- Per Serving: Calories: 190;Fat: 3g;Protein: 6g;Carbs: 36g.

Tofu Scramble

Servings: 4
Cooking Time: 50 Minutes

Ingredients:

- 8 oz extra firm tofu
- 2 tbsp olive oil
- 1 red bell pepper, chopped
- 1 tomato, finely chopped
- 2 tbsp chopped scallions
- Sea salt and pepper to taste
- 1 tsp red chili powder
- 3 tsp grated Parmesan cheese

Directions:

1. Place the tofu in between two parchment papers to drain liquid for about 30 minutes. Warm the olive oil in a large nonstick skillet until no longer foaming. Crumble the tofu into the skillet and fry until golden brown, stirring occasionally, making sure not to break the tofu into tiny pieces, about 4 to 6 minutes.

2. Stir in the bell pepper, tomato, scallions, and cook until the vegetables are soft, about 4 minutes. Then, season with salt, pepper, chili powder, and stir in the Parmesan cheese to incorporate and melt for about 2 minutes. Spoon the scramble into a serving platter and serve.

Nutrition Info:

- Per Serving: Calories: 130;Fat: 11g;Protein: 7g;Carbs: 4.8g.

Morning Matcha & Ginger Shake

Servings: 2
Cooking Time: 5 Minutes

Ingredients:

- 1 tbsp hemp seeds
- 1 tbsp grated ginger
- 2 tbsp honey
- 2 tbsp matcha powder
- 2 cups almond milk
- 1 cup ice

Directions:

1. Place the hemp seeds, ginger, honey, matcha, ice, and milk in a blender and pulse until smooth. Serve.

Nutrition Info:

- Per Serving: Calories: 350;Fat: 8g;Protein: 10g;Carbs: 57g.

Omelette With Smoky Shrimp

Servings: 2
Cooking Time: 15 Minutes

Ingredients:

- 6 large eggs
- 1½ teaspoons fine Himalayan salt, divided
- 1 teaspoon black pepper, ground
- 1 teaspoon liquid smoke
- ¼ cup Garlic Confit with oil
- ¾ to 1-pound large shrimp, peeled and deveined
- 2 teaspoons avocado oil, divided
- 1 cup arugula

Directions:

1. In a large mixing bowl, place the eggs, ½ teaspoon of the salt, the pepper, and the liquid smoke. Whisk until frothy, then set aside.

2. Heat a 6-inch skillet over medium heat. Place the confit in the skillet when it's hot, quickly followed by the shrimp. Add the remaining teaspoon of salt and for 2 to 3 minutes sauté until the shrimp are pink and begins to coil. Transfer everything from the skillet to a plate. Don't clean the pan.

3. Quickly add 1 teaspoon of the avocado oil, swirl it, and pour in half of the whisked eggs in the same skillet. Add 6 shrimp and half of the garlic, once the bottom is no longer translucent. For 4 to 5 minutes, cover the skillet with a tight-fitting lid and cook.

4. Remove the lid and pick up the skillet to swirl the contents around for 30 seconds. There will be a thin layer of the egg still fluid on the top, and moving it around like this will spread that layer out over the top of the omelet so it will finish cooking while leaving the omelet slightly moist.

5. Run a spatula along the edge of the omelet and slide it onto a plate. Put the skillet back on the stove and use the remaining ingredients to make the second omelet in the same way by adding the remaining teaspoon of avocado oil.

6. Top each omelet with ½ cup arugula and serve right away.

Nutrition Info:

- Per Serving: Calories: 403 ;Fat: 21g ;Protein: 42g;Carbs: 5g .

Blueberry Smoothie With Ginger

Servings: 2
Cooking Time: 10 Minutes

Ingredients:

- 1 cup fresh blueberries
- 2 cups almond milk
- 1 packet stevia
- 2 cups crushed ice
- 1-in piece fresh ginger, peeled and chopped

Directions:

1. Place the blueberries, almond milk, stevia, ginger, and ice in a blender and pulse until smooth. Serve right away.

Nutrition Info:

- Per Serving: Calories: 96;Fat: 4g;Protein: 4g;Carbs: 17g.

Choco-berry Smoothie

Servings: 2
Cooking Time: 10 Minutes

Ingredients:

- 1 tbsp poppy seeds
- 2 cups soy milk
- 2 cups blackberries
- 2 tbsp pure maple syrup
- 2 tbsp cocoa powder

Directions:

1. Submerge poppy seeds in soy milk and let sit for 5 minutes. Transfer to a food processor and add soy milk, blackberries, maple syrup, and cocoa powder. Blitz until smooth. Serve right away in glasses. Enjoy!

Nutrition Info:

- Per Serving: Calories: 288;Fat: 8g;Protein: 12g;Carbs: 47g.

Almond & Raisin Granola

Servings: 6
Cooking Time: 20 Minutes

Ingredients:

- 5 ½ cups old-fashioned oats
- 1 ½ cups chopped walnuts
- ½ cup sunflower seeds
- 1 cup golden raisins
- 1 cup shaved almonds
- 1 cup pure maple syrup
- ½ tsp ground cinnamon
- ¼ tsp ground allspice
- A pinch of sea salt

Directions:

1. Preheat your oven to 325ºF. In a baking dish, mix the oats, walnuts, and sunflower seeds. Bake for 10 minutes. Remove and stir in the raisins, almonds, maple syrup, cinnamon, allspice, and salt. Bake for an additional 15 minutes. Allow cooling completely. Serve and enjoy!

Nutrition Info:

- Per Serving: Calories: 791;Fat: 34g;Protein: 21g;Carbs: 111g.

Carrot-strawberry Smoothie

Servings: 2
Cooking Time: 5 Minutes

Ingredients:

- 1 cup diced carrots
- 1 cup strawberries
- 1 apple, chopped
- 2 tbsp maple syrup
- 2 cups almond milk

Directions:

1. Place in a food processor all the ingredients. Blitz until smooth. Pour in glasses and serve.

Nutrition Info:

- Per Serving: Calories: 708;Fat: 58g;Protein: 7g;Carbs: 53.4g.

No-bread Avocado Sandwich

Servings: 2
Cooking Time: 10 Minutes

Ingredients:

- 1 avocado, sliced
- 1 large red tomato, sliced
- 2 oz gem lettuce leaves
- 1 tsp almond butter, softened
- 1 oz tofu, sliced
- 1 tsp chopped parsley

Directions:

1. Put the avocado on a plate and place the tomato slices by the avocado. Arrange the lettuce on a flat plate to serve as the base of the sandwich.

2. To assemble the sandwich, smear each leaf of the lettuce with almond butter, and arrange some tofu slices in the leaves. Then, share the avocado and tomato slices on each cheese. Garnish with parsley and serve.

Nutrition Info:

- Per Serving: Calories: 273;Fat: 25g;Protein: 5g;Carbs: 12.6g.

Sauces, Condiments, And Dressings

Creamy Dressing With Sesame

Servings: ¾
Cooking Time: 0 Minutes

Ingredients:

- ½ cup canned coconut milk, full-fat
- 2 tablespoons tahini
- 2 tablespoons lime juice, freshly squeezed
- 1 teaspoon minced garlic, bottled
- 1 teaspoon fresh chives, minced
- Pinch sea salt

Directions:

1. Whisk in a small bowl the coconut milk, tahini, lime juice, garlic, and chives until well blended. You can also prepare this in a blender.
2. Season with sea salt and transfer the dressing to a container with a lid. Refrigerate for up to 1 week.

Nutrition Info:

- Per Serving: Calories: 40 ;Fat: 4g ;Protein: 1g;Carbs: 2g .

Old Fashioned Dressing With Lemon And Mustard

Servings: 1 ½
Cooking Time: 0 Minutes

Ingredients:

- 1 cup extra-virgin olive oil
- ¼ cup lemon juice, fresh
- 1 tablespoon honey
- 1 teaspoon Dijon mustard
- 1 shallot, sliced
- 1 teaspoon lemon zest, grated
- 1 teaspoon salt
- ¼ teaspoon pepper

Directions:

1. Combine the olive oil, lemon juice, honey, Dijon, shallot, lemon zest, salt, and pepper in a blender or food processor. Process until smooth.
2. Refrigerate in an airtight container for up to 5 days.

Nutrition Info:

- Per Serving: Calories: 180 ;Fat: 20g ;Protein: 16g;Carbs: 2g .

Fragrant Peach Butter

Servings: 2
Cooking Time: 3 Hours

Ingredients:

- Eight 3 pounds peaches, peeled, pitted, and chopped, or about 6 cups frozen, sliced peaches
- Water
- ¼ cup raw honey

Directions:

1. Combine in a large saucepan over high heat the peaches with enough water to cover the fruit by about 1 inch. Bring the liquid to a boil.

2. Reduce the heat to low and simmer for 3 hours while stirring frequently until the mixture appears a thick applesauce.

3. Stir in the honey. Simmer for 30 minutes until the mixture starts to caramelize. Remove the peach butter from the heat and let it cool for 30 minutes.

4. Spoon the mixture into a container and cool completely before covering. Keep refrigerated for up to 2 weeks.

Nutrition Info:

- Per Serving: Calories: 46 ;Fat: 15g;Protein: 1g;Carbs: 11g .

Garlicky Sauce With Tahini

Servings: 1
Cooking Time: 0 Minutes

Ingredients:

- ½ cup tahini
- 1 garlic clove, minced
- Juice of 1 lemon
- Zest of 1 lemon
- ½ teaspoon salt, plus additional as needed
- ½ cup warm water, plus additional as needed

Directions:

1. Stir together in a small bowl the tahini and garlic.

2. Add the lemon juice, lemon zest, and salt. Stir well.

3. Whisk in ½ cup of warm water, until fully mixed and creamy. Add more water if the sauce is too thick.

4. Taste and adjust the seasoning if needed.

5. Refrigerate in a sealed container.

Nutrition Info:

- Per Serving: Calories: 180 ;Fat: 16g ;Protein: 5g ;Carbs: 7g .

Commercial And Mild Curry Powder

Servings: ¼
Cooking Time: 0 Minutes

Ingredients:
- 1 tablespoon turmeric, ground
- 1 tablespoon cumin, ground
- 2 teaspoons coriander, ground
- 1 teaspoon cardamom, ground
- 1 teaspoon cinnamon, ground
- 1 teaspoon ginger, ground
- ½ teaspoon fenugreek powder
- ½ teaspoon cloves, ground

Directions:
1. Stir together in a small bowl the turmeric, cumin, coriander, cardamom, cinnamon, ginger, fenugreek, and cloves until fully blended.
2. Store the curry powder in an airtight container for up to 1 month.

Nutrition Info:
- Per Serving: Calories: 6 ;Fat: 15g;Protein: 46g;Carbs: 1g.

Caramelized Roasted Fennel With Sunflower Seed Pesto

Servings: 2
Cooking Time: 30 Minutes

Ingredients:
- 2 fennel bulbs
- 8 garlic cloves, peeled
- 2 tablespoons extra-virgin olive oil, plus additional as needed
- ¾ cup sunflower seeds
- ¼ cup lemon juice, freshly squeezed
- ½ teaspoon sea salt, plus additional as needed

Directions:
1. Preheat the oven to 350°F.
2. Trim the fronds from the fennel bulbs and set them aside. Cut off the stalks and save them. Halve the fennel bulbs, remove and discard the core. Chop the fennel roughly.
3. Combine the chopped fennel and garlic in a large roasting pan.
4. Drizzle with the olive oil and toss to coat.
5. Place the pan in the preheated oven and roast for 30 minutes while stirring halfway through. Remove the pan from the oven and cool.
6. Grind in a food processor the sunflower seeds into a rough meal.
7. Add the roasted fennel and garlic along with the lemon juice and sea salt. Process until everything comes together. Add an additional 1 or 2 tablespoons of olive oil, or water if the pesto is dry.
8. Roughly chop a handful of the reserved fennel fronds. Add them to the pesto. Pulse until combined. Taste and adjust the seasoning if needed.

Nutrition Info:
- Per Serving: Calories: 80 ;Fat: 6g ;Protein: 2g ;Carbs: 6g .

Dairy Free Apple Cider Vinegar With Tangy Barbecue Sauce

Servings: 2
Cooking Time: 3 To 4 Hours

Ingredients:

- 1¼ cups all-natural ketchup
- ¼ cup molasses
- ¼ cup coconut sugar
- 3 tablespoons apple cider vinegar
- 1 tablespoon Worcestershire sauce
- 1½ teaspoons garlic powder
- 1 teaspoon Dijon mustard
- ½ teaspoon sea salt
- ½ teaspoon onion powder
- Pinch cayenne pepper

Directions:

1. Combine the ketchup, molasses, coconut sugar, vinegar, Worcestershire sauce, garlic powder, mustard, salt, onion powder, and cayenne in your slow cooker.
2. Cover the cooker and set it to low. Cook for 3 to 4 hours.
3. Let cool and refrigerate in an airtight container.

Nutrition Info:

- Per Serving: Calories: 416 ;Fat: 15g;Protein: 46g;Carbs: 105g .

Delicious Pesto With Kale

Servings: 1
Cooking Time: 0 Minutes

Ingredients:

- 2 cups chopped kale leaves, thoroughly washed and stemmed
- ½ cup almonds, toasted
- 2 garlic cloves
- 3 tablespoons lemon juice, freshly squeezed
- 3 tablespoons extra-virgin olive oil
- 2 teaspoons lemon zest
- 1 teaspoon salt
- ½ teaspoon black pepper, freshly ground
- ¼ teaspoon red pepper flakes

Directions:

1. Combine in a food processor the kale, almonds, garlic, lemon juice, olive oil, lemon zest, salt, black pepper, and red pepper flakes then process until smooth.
2. Refrigerate in an airtight container for up to one week.

Nutrition Info:

- Per Serving: Calories: 91 ;Fat: 8g ;Protein: 2g;Carbs: 4g .

To Die For Homemade Mayonnaise

Servings: 1
Cooking Time: 0 Minutes

Ingredients:

- 3 tablespoons coconut vinegar
- 1 teaspoon thyme leaves, dried
- ½ teaspoon garlic, granulated
- ½ teaspoon mustard, dry
- ½ teaspoon Himalayan salt, fine
- 3 large egg yolks
- 1 cup avocado oil

Directions:

1. Place the vinegar and seasonings in a 16 ounces measuring cup or quart-sized mason jar. Add gently the egg yolks and the avocado oil.

2. Insert the immersion blender into the mixture and turn it on high then move it up and down slightly until the mix is completely emulsified. Scrape all of the mayonnaise off of the blender by using a spatula and then transfer the mayonnaise to a jar or other container with a tight-fitting lid.

3. Store in the refrigerator for up to 10 days.

Nutrition Info:

- Per Serving: Calories: 262 ;Fat: 30g ;Protein: 1g;Carbs: 4g.

Traditional And Delightful Gremolata Sauce

Servings: 1
Cooking Time: 0 Minutes

Ingredients:

- ¾ cup finely fresh parsley, chopped
- Juice of 2 lemons or 6 tablespoons
- Zest of 2 lemons
- 2 tablespoons olive oil
- 2 teaspoons minced garlic, bottled
- ¼ teaspoon sea salt

Directions:

1. Stir together in a small bowl the parsley, lemon juice, lemon zest, olive oil, garlic, and sea salt until well blended.

2. Refrigerate in a sealed container for up to 4 days.

Nutrition Info:

- Per Serving: Calories: 33 ;Fat: 4g ;Protein: 46g;Carbs: 1g.

Game Changer Pickled Red Onions

Servings: 4
Cooking Time: 10 Minutes

Ingredients:

- 2 cups water, filtered
- 1 cup apple cider vinegar
- 1 teaspoon Himalayan salt, fine
- 1 teaspoon granulated erythritol or another low-carb sweetener
- 2 bay leaves
- 2 red onions, thinly sliced and cut into half-moons

Directions:

1. Combine the water, vinegar, salt, erythritol, and bay leaves in a small saucepan over medium heat. Bring to a light simmer and cook for 8 minutes. Stir to make sure the salt and sweetener have dissolved.

2. In a jar, put all the onion slices with the bay leaves and then pour the hot brine over the onions until fully submerged. Let the onions steep for 30 minutes at room temperature before using. Seal the jar and store it in the fridge for up to a month.

Nutrition Info:

- Per Serving: Calories: 5 ;Fat: 7g ;Protein: 6g;Carbs: 2g

Decadent And Simple Alfredo With Cauliflower

Servings: 2
Cooking Time: 12 Minutes

Ingredients:

- 3 cups cauliflower, florets
- 5 cloves garlic, peeled
- 1 cup coconut milk, full-fat
- 3 tablespoons salted butter, ghee, or lard
- 1 tablespoon fish sauce
- 1 tablespoon red wine vinegar
- 1 teaspoon Himalayan salt, fine
- 1 teaspoon black pepper, ground

Directions:

1. Fill a saucepan with about an inch of water and add the cauliflower and garlic. Heat the pan over medium-high heat and bring to a boil with the lid on. Cook for 8 minutes until the cauliflower is fork-tender. Remove from the heat and drain.
2. In a blender, place the cauliflower, garlic, and remaining ingredients. Purée until smooth.
3. Store in an airtight container in the fridge for up to 10 days. Bring to a simmer in a saucepan over medium heat to reheat.

Nutrition Info:

- Per Serving: Calories: 250 ;Fat: 24g ;Protein: 4g ;Carbs: 9g .

Satisfying And Thick Dressing With Avocado

Servings: 2
Cooking Time: 0 Minutes

Ingredients:

- 1 ripe avocado
- 1 cup coconut yogurt, plain
- ¼ cup lemon juice, freshly squeezed
- 1 scallion, chopped
- 1 tablespoon fresh cilantro, chopped

Directions:

1. Blend in a food processor the avocado, yogurt, lemon juice, scallion, and cilantro until smooth.
2. Refrigerate in an airtight container.

Nutrition Info:

- Per Serving: Calories: 33 ;Fat: 3g ;Protein: 8g;Carbs: 2g .

Tricky Cheesy Yellow Sauce

Servings: 2
Cooking Time: 0 Minutes

Ingredients:

- 1½ cups steamed, mashed cauliflower florets and hot
- ½ cup coconut milk, full-fat
- ½ cup nutritional yeast
- 1 tablespoon unsalted butter, ghee, or lard
- 1½ teaspoons coconut vinegar
- 1 teaspoon Himalayan salt, fine
- 1 teaspoon garlic powder

Directions:

1. Place all of the ingredients in a blender. Cover and blend on low, slowly bringing the speed up to high.
2. Continue to blend until the sauce is completely smooth. Taste for seasoning and add a little more salt and/or garlic powder if you like.
3. Store in an airtight container in the refrigerator for up to a week. Warm in a saucepan on the stovetop over medium heat and stir occasionally.

Nutrition Info:

- Per Serving: Calories: 185 ;Fat: 11g ;Protein: 11g;Carbs: 15g .

Fresh Maple Dressing

Servings: 1 ¼
Cooking Time: 0 Minutes

Ingredients:

- 1 cup canned coconut milk, full-fat
- 2 tablespoons pure maple syrup
- 1 tablespoon Dijon mustard
- 1 tablespoon apple cider vinegar
- Sea salt

Directions:

1. Whisk the coconut milk, maple syrup, mustard, and cider vinegar in a medium bowl until smoothly blended. Season with sea salt.
2. Refrigerate the dressing in a sealed container for up to 1 week.

Nutrition Info:

- Per Serving: Calories: 67 ;Fat: 6g ;Protein: 1g;Carbs: 4g.

Natural Dressing With Ginger And Turmeric

Servings: ½
Cooking Time: 0 Minutes

Ingredients:

- 1 cup extra-virgin olive oil
- ¼ cup apple cider vinegar
- ½ teaspoon Dijon mustard
- 1 garlic clove, sliced
- ½ teaspoon fresh ginger root, minced
- 1 teaspoon salt
- ½ teaspoon turmeric, ground
- ¼ teaspoon coriander, ground
- ¼ teaspoon black pepper, freshly ground

Directions:

1. Combine all the ingredients in a blender or food processor and process until smooth.
2. Refrigerate in an airtight container for up to a week.

Nutrition Info:

- Per Serving: Calories: 160 ;Fat: 18g; Protein: 46g;Carbs: 4g.

Salads

Arugula Salad With Salmon

Servings: 2
Cooking Time: 15 Minutes

Ingredients:

- 1 tbsp lemon juice
- 1 skinless salmon fillet
- 3 tbsp extra-virgin olive oil
- Black pepper to taste
- 1 cup cherry tomatoes, halved
- 4 cups arugula leaves
- ½ cup sliced red onion
- 1 tbsp balsamic vinegar

Directions:

1. Rub the salmon with some olive oil, lemon juice, and pepper. Heat 1 tbsp of olive oil in a skillet over medium heat and cook the salmon, skin-side down, for 6-8 minutes or until cooked through, turning once. Remove and let it cool, then flake it. Place the arugula, onion, and cherry tomatoes in a salad bowl. Add the remaining olive oil and balsamic vinegar and toss to coat. Top the salad with fish and serve.

Nutrition Info:

- Per Serving: Calories: 570;Fat: 29g;Protein: 66g;Carbs: 9g.

Spinach & Pomegranate Salad

Servings: 4
Cooking Time: 10 Minutes

Ingredients:

- 2 tbsp extra-virgin olive oil
- 4 cups fresh baby spinach
- ¼ cup pomegranate seeds
- ¼ cup raspberry vinaigrette

Directions:

1. Mix the spinach and walnuts in a bowl. Sprinkle with olive oil and raspberry vinaigrette and toss to combine.

Nutrition Info:

- Per Serving: Calories: 500;Fat: 49g;Protein: 12g;Carbs: 10g.

Fragrant Coconut Fruit Salad

Servings: 4
Cooking Time:0 Minutes

Ingredients:

- Dressing:
- ¾ cup canned lite coconut milk
- 2 tablespoons almond butter
- 2 tablespoons lime juice, freshly squeezed
- Salad:
- 6 cups mixed greens
- ½ pineapple, peeled, cored, and diced, or 3 cups precut packaged pineapple
- 1 mango, peeled, pitted, and diced, or 2 cups frozen chunks, thawed
- 1 cup quartered strawberries, fresh
- 1 cup (1 inch) green bean pieces
- ½ cup shredded coconut, unsweetened
- 1 tablespoon fresh basil, chopped

Directions:

1. Whisk the coconut milk, almond butter, and lime juice in a small bowl until smooth. Set it aside.
2. Toss the mixed greens with three-fourths of the dressing in a large bowl. Arrange the salad on four plates.
3. Toss the pineapple, mango, strawberries, and green beans in the same bowl with the remaining fourth of the dressing.
4. Top each salad with the fruit and vegetable mixture and serve garnished with the coconut and basil.

Nutrition Info:

- Per Serving: Calories: 311| Fat: 19g ;Protein: 5g;Carbs: 36g .

Summer Time Sizzling Green Salad With Salmon

Servings: 2
Cooking Time: 10 Minutes

Ingredients:

- 2 salmon fillets, skinless
- 2 cups of seasonal greens
- ½ cup zucchini, sliced
- 1 tablespoon balsamic vinegar
- 2 tablespoons extra virgin olive oil
- 2 sprigs thyme, torn from the stem
- 1 lemon, juiced

Directions:

1. Preheat the broiler to a medium-high heat.
2. For 10 minutes, broil the salmon in parchment paper with some oil, lemon, and pepper.
3. Slice the zucchini and sauté for 4-5 minutes with the oil in a pan on medium heat.
4. Build the salad by creating a bed of zucchini and topping it with flaked salmon.
5. Drizzle with balsamic vinegar and sprinkle with thyme.

Nutrition Info:

- Per Serving: Calories: 67 ;Fat: 6g ;Protein: 7g;Carbs: 3g .

Minty Eggplant Salad

Servings: 2
Cooking Time: 45 Minutes

Ingredients:

- 1 lemon, half zested and juiced, half cut into wedges
- 1 tsp olive oil
- 1 eggplant, chopped
- ½ tsp ground cumin
- ½ tsp ground ginger
- ¼ tsp turmeric
- ¼ tsp ground nutmeg
- Sea salt to taste
- 2 tbsp capers
- 1 tbsp chopped green olives
- 1 garlic clove, pressed
- 2 tbsp fresh mint, chopped
- 2 cups watercress, chopped

Directions:

1. In a skillet over medium heat, warm the oil. Place the eggplant and cook for 5 minutes. Add in cumin, ginger, turmeric, nutmeg, and salt. Cook for another 10 minutes. Stir in lemon zest, lemon juice, capers, olives, garlic, and mint. Cook for 1-2 minutes more. Place some watercress on each plate and top with the eggplant mixture. Serve.

Nutrition Info:

- Per Serving: Calories: 110;Fat: 3g;Protein: 44g;Carbs: 20g.

Convenient Salad With Raspberry Vinaigrette, Spinach, And Walnut

Servings: 4
Cooking Time: 0 Minutes

Ingredients:

- 4 cups baby spinach, fresh
- ¼ cup walnut pieces
- ¼ cup raspberry vinaigrette

Directions:

1. Combine the spinach and walnuts in a medium bowl.
2. Toss with the vinaigrette and serve immediately.

Nutrition Info:

- Per Serving: Calories: 501 ;Fat: 50g ;Carbs: 9g ;Sugar: 2g ;Fiber: 5g ;Protein: 11g ;Sodium: 96mg

Mango Rice Salad With Lime Dressing

Servings: 4
Cooking Time: 15 Minutes

Ingredients:

- ½ cup chopped roasted peanuts
- 3 ½ cups cooked brown rice
- 1 mango, sliced
- 4 green onions, chopped
- 3 tbsp fresh lime juice
- 2 tsp agave nectar
- 1 tsp grated fresh ginger
- 1/3 cup grapeseed oil
- Sea salt and pepper to taste

Directions:

1. In a bowl, mix the rice, peanuts, mango, and green onions. Set aside. In another bowl, whisk the lime juice, agave nectar, and ginger. Add oil, salt, and pepper and stir to combine. Pour over the rice and toss to coat. Serve.

Nutrition Info:

- Per Serving: Calories: 490;Fat: 29g;Protein: 10g;Carbs: 50g.

Carrot Salad With Cherries & Pecans

Servings: 4
Cooking Time: 15 Minutes

Ingredients:

- 1 lb carrots, shredded
- 1 cup dried cherries, sliced
- 2 ½ cups toasted pecans
- 3 tbsp fresh lemon juice
- 3 tbsp avocado oil
- Sea salt and pepper to taste

Directions:

1. Combine the carrots, cherries, and pecans in a bowl. In another bowl, mix the lemon juice, avocado oil, salt, and pepper. Pour over the salad and toss to coat. Serve.

Nutrition Info:

- Per Serving: Calories: 595;Fat: 55g;Protein: 8g;Carbs: 27g.

All Green Salad With Basil-cherry Dressing

Servings: 4
Cooking Time: 25 Minutes

Ingredients:

- ¼ cup olive oil
- ½ cup pitted cherries
- 2 tbsp lemon juice
- 2 tbsp raw honey
- 1 tsp chopped fresh basil
- Sea salt to taste
- 5 oz blanched broccoli florets
- 2 cups mixed greens
- 1 cup snow peas
- ½ cucumber, sliced
- 2 green onions, thinly sliced

Directions:

1. Combine the cherries, olive oil, lemon juice, honey, salt, and basil in your food processor and pulse until smooth. Add the broccoli, mixed greens, snow peas, cucumber, and green onions to a salad bowl. Coat with dressing.

Nutrition Info:

- Per Serving: Calories: 190;Fat: 15g;Protein: 3g;Carbs: 18g.

Cucumber & Pear Rice Salad

Servings: 4
Cooking Time: 15 Minutes

Ingredients:

- 1 cup brown rice
- ¼ cup olive oil
- ¼ cup orange juice
- 1 pear, cored and diced
- ½ cucumber, diced
- ¼ cup raisins
- Sea salt and pepper to taste

Directions:

1. Place the rice in a pot with 2 cups of salted water. Bring to a boil, then lower the heat and simmer for 15 minutes. In a bowl, whisk together the olive oil, orange juice, salt, and pepper. Stir in the pear, cucumber, raisins, and cooked rice. Serve.

Nutrition Info:

- Per Serving: Calories: 355;Fat: 15g;Protein: 1g;Carbs: 52g.

Out Of This World Salad With Basil And Tomato

Servings: 4
Cooking Time: 0 Minutes

Ingredients:

- 4 large heirloom tomatoes, chopped
- ¼ cup fresh basil leaves, torn
- 2 garlic cloves, finely minced
- ¼ cup extra-virgin olive oil
- ½ teaspoon sea salt
- ¼ teaspoon black pepper, freshly ground

Directions:

1. Gently mix together the tomatoes, basil, garlic, olive oil, salt, and pepper in a medium bowl.
2. Serve and enjoy.

Nutrition Info:

- Per Serving: Calories: 140 ;Fat: 14g ;Protein: 1g ;Carbs: 4g .

Superb Salad With Chickpea

Servings: 4
Cooking Time: 20 Minutes

Ingredients:

- 1 large bunch kale, thoroughly washed, stemmed, and cut into thin strips
- 2 teaspoons lemon juice, freshly squeezed
- 2 tablespoons extra-virgin olive oil, divided
- ¾ teaspoon sea salt, divided
- 2 cups cooked chickpeas, 14-oz
- 1 teaspoon sweet paprika

Directions:

1. Combine the kale, lemon juice, 1 tablespoon of olive oil, and ¼ teaspoon of salt in a large bowl.
2. Massage with your hands the kale for 5 minutes, or until it starts to wilt and becomes bright green and shiny.
3. Add the remaining 1 tablespoon of olive oil to a skillet set over medium-low heat.
4. Stir in the chickpeas, paprika, and remaining ½ teaspoon of salt. Cook for about 15 minutes, or until warm. The chickpeas might start to crisp in spots.
5. Pour the chickpeas over the kale. Toss well.
6. Serve immediately.

Nutrition Info:

- Per Serving: Calories: 359 ;Fat: 20g ;Protein: 13g ;Carbs: 35g .

Spinach Salad With Cranberries

Servings: 1
Cooking Time: 10 Minutes

Ingredients:

- 1 cup chopped fresh cranberries
- 1 tbsp apple cider vinegar
- 2 tsp olive oil
- 1 orange, sliced
- 1 cup spinach, chopped
- 2 tsp grated ginger

Directions:

1. Combine the vinegar and olive oil in a bowl. Add the cranberries, spinach, ginger, and orange and toss to coat. Chill before serving.

Nutrition Info:

- Per Serving: Calories: 300;Fat: 19g;Protein: 2g;Carbs: 30g.

Summer Salad

Servings: 4
Cooking Time: 25 Minutes

Ingredients:

- 1 Lebanese cucumber, cubed
- 4 cups watermelon cubes
- 1 cup snow peasp halved
- 1 scallion, chopped
- 2 cups shredded kale
- 1 tbsp chopped cilantro
- ½ lime, zested and juiced
- ½ cup olive oil
- 2 tbsp honey
- Sea salt to taste

Directions:

1. Whisk the olive oil, lime zest, lime juice, honey, and salt in a bowl. Add the watermelon, cucumber, snow peas, scallion, and toss to coat. Top with the watermelon mixture. Serve garnished with cilantro.

Nutrition Info:

- Per Serving: Calories: 350;Fat: 25g;Protein: 3g;Carbs: 30g.

African Zucchini Salad

Servings: 2
Cooking Time: 20 Minutes

Ingredients:

- 1 lemon, half zested and juiced, half cut into wedges
- 1 tsp olive oil
- 1 zucchini, chopped
- ½ tsp ground cumin
- ½ tsp ground ginger
- ¼ tsp turmeric
- ¼ tsp ground nutmeg
- A pinch of sea salt
- 2 tbsp capers
- 1 tbsp chopped green olives
- 1 garlic clove, pressed
- 2 tbsp fresh mint, chopped
- 2 cups spinach, chopped

Directions:

1. Warm the olive oil in a skillet over medium heat. Place the zucchini and sauté for 10 minutes. Stir in cumin, ginger, turmeric, nutmeg, and salt. Pour in lemon zest, lemon juice, capers, garlic, and mint and cook for 2 minutes more. Divide the spinach between serving plates and top with zucchini mixture. Garnish with lemon and olives.

Nutrition Info:

- Per Serving: Calories: 50;Fat: 3g;Protein: 41g;Carbs: 5g.

Nutritious Bowl With Lentil, Vegetable, And Fruit

Servings: 4 To 6
Cooking Time: 0 Minutes

Ingredients:

- 1 cup red lentils
- 2 cups water
- 4 cups cooked brown rice
- One 15 ounces can lentils, drained and rinsed
- Chicken Lettuce Wraps sauce
- 1 head radicchio, cored and torn into pieces, divided
- 1 small jicama, peeled and cut into thin sticks, divided
- 2 red Bartlett ripe pears, cored, quartered, and sliced, divided
- 2 scallions, sliced, divided

Directions:

1. Combine the red lentils and the water in a medium bowl. Cover and refrigerate overnight. Drain the lentils when ready to prepare the salad.

2. Combine the brown rice and canned lentils in a medium bowl. Stir in half of the Chicken Lettuce Wraps sauce. Let the mixture stand for 30 minutes, or overnight.

3. Divide the lentil-rice mixture among serving bowls. Top each bowl with equal amounts of the soaked and drained red lentils. Garnish each serving with the radicchio, jicama, pears, and scallions.

4. Drizzle each with some of the remaining Chicken Lettuce Wraps sauce.

Nutrition Info:

- Per Serving: Calories: 989 ;Fat: 31g ;Protein: 31g ;Carbs: 151g .

Vegetarian Mains

Habanero Pinto Bean & Bell Pepper Pot

Servings: 6
Cooking Time: 20 Minutes

Ingredients:

- 1 tsp olive oil
- 2 red bell peppers, diced
- 1 habanero pepper, minced
- 2 cans pinto beans
- ½ cup vegetable broth
- 1 tsp ground cumin
- 1 tsp chili powder
- Sea salt and pepper to taste

Directions:

1. Heat the oil in a pot over medium heat. Place in bell and habanero peppers. Sauté for 5 minutes until tender. Add beans, broth, cumin, chili powder, salt, and pepper. Bring to a boil, then lower the heat and simmer for 10 minutes.

Nutrition Info:

- Per Serving: Calories: 135;Fat: 2g;Protein: 7g;Carbs: 23g.

Homemade Burgers With Bean And Yam

Servings: 4 To 6
Cooking Time: 35 Minutes

Ingredients:

- 1 cup rolled oats, gluten-free
- 3 cups cooked navy beans, 1½ cups dried
- 2 cups yam/sweet potato purée, about 2 yams/sweet potatoes, steamed and mashed
- ½ cup sunflower seed butter, or tahini
- 1 tablespoon fresh ginger, grated
- ½ teaspoon salt

Directions:

1. Pulse the oats in a food processor a few times until a rough meal form.
2. Add the beans, yam purée, sunflower seed butter, ginger, and salt. Blend until well mixed. You can make this completely smooth, or leave it slightly chunky.
3. For 30 minutes, refrigerate the mixture to be firm.
4. Preheat the oven to 350°F.
5. Line a baking sheet with parchment paper or Silpat.
6. Scoop the mixture onto the prepared sheet using a �?cup or ½-cup measure. Gently pat the mixture down so the patties are 1 inch thick. Makes about 12 patties.
7. Place the sheet in the preheated oven and bake for 35 minutes. Flip the burgers halfway through the cooking time.

Nutrition Info:

- Per Serving: Calories: 581 ;Fat: 19g ;Protein: 27g ;Carbs: 81g .

Appetizing Casserole With Broccoli And Bean

Servings: 4
Cooking Time: 35 To 45 Minutes

Ingredients:

- ¾ cup vegetable broth, or water
- 2 broccoli heads, crowns and stalks finely chopped
- 1 teaspoon salt
- 2 cups cooked pinto or navy beans, or One 14 ounces can
- 1 to 2 tablespoons brown rice flour, or arrowroot flour
- 1 cup walnuts, chopped

Directions:

1. Preheat the oven to 350°F.
2. Warm the broth in a large ovenproof pot set over medium heat.
3. Add the broccoli and salt. Cook for 6 to 8 minutes, or until the broccoli is bright green.
4. Stir in the pinto beans and brown rice flour. Cook for 5 minutes more, or until the liquid thickens slightly.
5. Sprinkle the walnuts over the top.

Nutrition Info:

- Per Serving: Calories: 410 ;Fat: 20g ;Protein: 22g ;Carbs: 43g.

Teriyaki Vegetable Stir-fry

Servings: 4
Cooking Time: 25 Minutes

Ingredients:

- 2 tbsp olive oil
- 2 red bell peppers, chopped
- 1 onion, chopped
- 1 carrot, chopped
- 2 tbsp teriyaki sauce

Directions:

1. Warm the olive oil in a skillet over medium heat and place in bell peppers, onion, and carrot and cook for 5-7 minutes until the veggies are soft and golden brown. Mix the teriyaki sauce, pour it over the veggies, and cook for 3-4 minutes until the sauce thickens. Serve immediately.

Nutrition Info:

- Per Serving: Calories: 170;Fat: 11g;Protein: 3g;Carbs: 18g.

Pressure Cooked Ratatouille

Servings: 4
Cooking Time: 20 Minutes

Ingredients:

- 1 zucchini, sliced
- 2 tomatoes, sliced
- 1 tbsp balsamic vinegar
- 1 eggplant, sliced
- 1 onion, sliced
- 1 tbsp dried thyme
- 2 tbsp olive oil
- 2 garlic cloves, minced

Directions:

1. Add the garlic to a springform pan. Arrange the veggies in a circle. Sprinkle them with thyme and drizzle with olive oil. Pour 1 cup of water in your Instant Pot. Place the pan inside. Close the lid and cook for 10 minutes on "Manual" on high pressure. Let the steam release naturally for about 10 minutes. Serve immediately.

Nutrition Info:

- Per Serving: Calories: 105;Fat: 7g;Protein: 2g;Carbs: 10g.

Soft Zucchini With White Beans And Olives Stuffing

Servings: 4
Cooking Time: 20 Minutes

Ingredients:

- 4 large zucchinis, halved lengthwise
- 2 tablespoons extra-virgin olive oil, plus additional for brushing
- ½ teaspoon salt, plus additional for seasoning
- Freshly ground black pepper
- Pinch ground rosemary
- One 15 ounces can white beans, drained and rinsed
- ½ cup pitted green olives, chopped
- 2 garlic cloves, minced
- 1 cup arugula, coarsely chopped
- ¼ cup fresh parsley, chopped
- 1 tablespoon apple cider vinegar

Directions:

1. Preheat the oven to 375°F.
2. Brush a rimmed baking sheet with olive oil.
3. Carefully scoop out using a small spoon or melon baller and discard the seeds from the zucchini halves.
4. Brush the scooped-out section of each zucchini boat with olive oil and lightly season the inside of each boat with salt, pepper, and rosemary.
5. Transfer the zucchini to the prepared baking sheet, cut-side up. Place the sheet in the preheated oven and roast for 15 to 20 minutes, or until the zucchini are tender and lightly browned.
6. Lightly mash in a medium bowl the white beans with a fork.
7. Add the olives, garlic, arugula, parsley, cider vinegar, the remaining ½ teaspoon of salt, and the remaining 2 tablespoons of olive oil. Season with pepper and mix well.
8. Spoon the bean mixture into the zucchini boats and serve.

Nutrition Info:

- Per Serving: Calories: 269| Fat: 12g ;Protein: 13g ;Carbs: 38g.

Favourite Pizza With Quinoa Flatbread

Servings: 4 To 6
Cooking Time: 40 Minutes

Ingredients:

- 1 Quinoa Flatbread
- 1 cup pearl onions, halved
- 2 tablespoons extra-virgin olive oil
- 2 cups arugula
- 1 can artichoke hearts in water, 14 ounces

Directions:

1. Prepare the flatbread according to the recipe's instructions. Remove it from the oven when the flatbread is done and increase the heat to 375°F.
2. Toss together the pearl onions and olive oil in a small baking dish.
3. Place the dish in the preheated oven and roast for 10 minutes.
4. Scatter the onions over the crust.
5. Top with the arugula and artichoke hearts.
6. Place the pizza back in the oven and bake for 12 minutes.
7. Cool the pizza slightly before slicing and serving.

Nutrition Info:

- Per Serving: Calories: 181 ;Fat: 13g Protein: 4g ;;Carbs: 13g.

Traditional Cilantro Pilaf

Servings: 6
Cooking Time: 30 Minutes

Ingredients:

- 3 tbsp extra-virgin olive oil
- 1 onion, minced
- 1 carrot, chopped
- 2 garlic cloves, minced
- 1 cup wild rice
- 1 ½ tsp ground fennel seeds
- ½ tsp ground cumin
- Sea salt and pepper to taste
- 3 tbsp minced cilantro

Directions:

1. Heat the oil in a pot over medium heat. Add onion, carrot, and garlic and sauté for 5 minutes. Stir in rice, fennel seeds, cumin, and 2 cups of water. Bring to a boil, then lower the heat and simmer for 20 minutes. Remove and fluff with a fork. Top with cilantro and black pepper.

Nutrition Info:

- Per Serving: Calories: 170;Fat: 7g;Protein: 5g;Carbs: 24g.

Vegetable & Hummus Pizza

Servings: 4
Cooking Time: 30 Minutes

Ingredients:

- 10 mushrooms, sliced
- 3 ½ cups whole-wheat flour
- 1 tsp yeast
- 1 tsp sea salt
- 1 pinch sugar
- 3 tbsp olive oil
- 1 cup hummus
- ½ cup baby spinach
- 16 cherry tomatoes, halved
- ½ cup sliced black olives
- ½ medium onion, sliced
- 2 tsp dried oregano

Directions:

1. Preheat your oven the 350ºF and lightly grease a pizza pan with cooking spray. In a medium bowl, mix the flour, nutritional yeast, salt, sugar, olive oil, and 1 cup warm water until smooth dough forms. Allow rising for an hour or until the dough doubles in size. Spread the dough on the pizza pan and apply the hummus to the dough. Add the mushrooms, spinach, tomatoes, olives, onion, and top with the oregano. Bake for 20 minutes. Cool for 5 minutes, slice, and serve.

Nutrition Info:

- Per Serving: Calories: 600;Fat: 20g;Protein: 18g;Carbs: 94g.

Chinese Fried Rice

Servings: 4
Cooking Time: 20 Minutes

Ingredients:

- 2 tbsp coconut oil
- 1 onion, chopped
- 1 large carrot, chopped
- 1 head broccoli, cut into florets
- 2 garlic cloves, minced
- 2 tsp grated fresh ginger
- 3 green onions, minced
- 3 ½ cups cooked brown rice
- 1 cup frozen peas, thawed
- 4 tsp low-sodium soy sauce
- 2 tsp dry white wine
- 1 tbsp extra-virgin olive oil

Directions:

1. Heat the coconut oil in a skillet over medium heat. Place in onion, carrot, and broccoli, sauté for 5 minutes until tender. Add in garlic, ginger, and green onions and sauté for another 3 minutes. Stir in rice, peas, soy sauce, and white wine and cook for 5 minutes. Add in olive oil, toss to combine. Serve right away.

Nutrition Info:

- Per Serving: Calories: 330;Fat: 12g;Protein: 3g;Carbs: 48g.

Peanuty Sugar Snaps With Lime And Satay Tofu

Servings: 2
Cooking Time: 15 Minutes

Ingredients:

- 1 pack of drained, pressed, and cubed tofu
- 3 tablespoons coconut oil
- a pinch of black pepper
- Sauce:
- 3 tablespoons soybean milk
- 1 tablespoon whole almond butter
- 2 tablespoons oyster sauce, reduced-sodium
- 1 tablespoon garlic powder
- 1 teaspoon chili flakes
- 1 teaspoon tomato purée
- 1 teaspoon lime juice
- 1 cup udon noodles/brown rice, cooked
- 1 cup of sugar snap peas

Directions:

1. Heat the oil on a high heat and then sauté the tofu until brown on each side.
2. Place onto paper towels to soak excess moisture and place to one side.
3. Heat the milk in a pan over medium heat until it starts to bubble and add the peanut butter and the rest of the ingredients for the sauce while stirring continuously for 5 minutes until smooth and hot.
4. Add the tofu to the sauce, cook for 4-5 minutes until heated through.
5. Steam or boil your sugar snap peas for 3-4 minutes.
6. Serve ingredients hot with your choice of cooked udon noodles or brown rice.

Nutrition Info:

- Per Serving: Calories: 394 ;Fat: 26g ;Protein: 8g ;Carbs: 36g .

Watercress & Mushroom Spaghetti

Servings: 4
Cooking Time: 30 Minutes

Ingredients:

- ½ lb chopped button mushrooms
- 1 lb whole-wheat spaghetti
- 2 tbsp olive oil
- 2 shallots, chopped
- 2 garlic cloves, minced
- 4 tsp low-sodium soy sauce
- 1 tsp hot sauce
- A handful of watercress
- ¼ cup chopped parsley
- Sea salt and pepper to taste

Directions:

1. Cook spaghetti in lightly salted water in a large pot over medium heat until al dente, 10 minutes. Drain and set aside. Heat the olive oil in a skillet and sauté shallots, garlic, and mushrooms for 5 minutes. Stir in soy sauce, and hot sauce. Cook for 1 minute. Toss spaghetti in the sauce along with watercress and parsley. Season with black pepper. Dish the food and serve warm.

Nutrition Info:

- Per Serving: Calories: 485;Fat: 9g;Protein: 13g;Carbs: 90g.

Seitan Cauliflower Gratin

Servings: 4
Cooking Time: 40 Minutes

Ingredients:

- 2 tbsp olive oil
- 1 leek, coarsely chopped
- 1 white onion, chopped
- 2 cups broccoli florets
- 1 cup cauliflower florets
- 2 cups crumbled seitan
- 1 cup coconut cream
- 2 tbsp mustard powder
- 5 oz grated Parmesan
- 4 tbsp fresh rosemary
- Sea salt and pepper to taste

Directions:

1. Preheat your oven to 450°F. Warm the olive oil in a pan over medium heat. Add the leek, white onion, broccoli, and cauliflower and cook for about 6 minutes. Transfer the vegetables to a baking dish. In the same pan, cook the seitan until browned. Mix the coconut cream and mustard powder in a bowl. Pour the mixture over the vegetables. Scatter the seitan and Parmesan cheese on top and sprinkle with rosemary, salt, and pepper. Bake for 15 minutes. Cool for a few minutes and serve.

Nutrition Info:

- Per Serving: Calories: 605;Fat: 39g;Protein: 19g;Carbs: 37g.

Magical One-pot Tomato Basil Pasta

Servings: 4
Cooking Time: 10 Minutes

Ingredients:

- 2 tablespoons extra-virgin olive oil, plus additional for drizzling
- 1 onion, sliced thin
- 2 garlic cloves, sliced thin
- 1 pound penne pasta, gluten-free
- One 15 ounces can tomatoes, chopped
- 1½ teaspoons salt
- ¼ teaspoon black pepper, freshly ground
- ¼ cup chopped fresh basil, plus 4 whole basil leaves
- 4½ cups water

Directions:

1. Heat 2 tablespoons of olive oil in a large, heavy-bottomed Dutch oven over medium heat. Add the onion and garlic. Stir to coat with the oil.

2. Add the pasta, tomatoes, salt, pepper, the 4 whole basil leaves, and water to the pot. Bring the liquid to a boil and cover the pot. Cook for 8 to 10 minutes. Check the pasta to see if it is cooked and add more water if necessary. Cook until the pasta is tender.

3. Transfer the pasta to a serving bowl and garnish with the remaining ¼ cup of chopped basil and a drizzle of olive oil.

Nutrition Info:

- Per Serving: Calories: 518 ;Fat: 11g ;Protein: 10g ;Carbs: 95g.

Spicy And Tasty Indian Cauliflower And Broccoli Rabe

Servings: 4
Cooking Time: 25 Minutes

Ingredients:

- 12 bunch broccoli rabe, rapini
- ½ cauliflower, florets
- 1 onion, diced
- 1 thumb-sized piece of ginger, minced
- 4 garlic cloves, minced
- 1 teaspoon black mustard seeds
- 1 teaspoon cumin seeds
- ½ teaspoon turmeric
- 1 teaspoon cumin powder
- ½ teaspoon coriander powder
- ½ teaspoon red chili flakes
- a pinch of black pepper
- 2 tablespoons coconut oil
- 1 tablespoon fresh cilantro, chopped

Directions:

1. Add the oil and heat on medium heat in a skillet.
2. Add the black mustard seeds, cumin seeds, and the spices and stir for 4 to 5 minutes.
3. Add the onions and stir for 5 minutes more or until softened.
4. Add the ginger, garlic, and red chili flakes, stirring for 5 minutes more then add in the rest of the spices.
5. Let the spices sink in for 5 minutes and add in the broccoli rabe and cauliflower.
6. Stir until the greens are covered in the spices and then reduce the heat and sauté for 5 to 6 minutes.
7. Garnish with cilantro and add pepper to taste and serve.

Nutrition Info:

- Per Serving: Calories: 519 ;Fat: 14g ;Protein: 51g ;Carbs: 46g.

Cheesy Cauliflower Casserole

Servings: 4
Cooking Time: 35 Minutes

Ingredients:

- 1 white onion, chopped
- ½ celery stalk, chopped
- 1 green bell pepper, chopped
- Sea salt and pepper to taste
- 1 head cauliflower, chopped
- 1 cup paleo mayonnaise
- 4 oz grated Parmesan
- 1 tsp red chili flakes

Directions:

1. Preheat your oven to 400ºF. Season onion, celery, and bell pepper with salt and black pepper. In a bowl, mix cauliflower, mayonnaise, Parmesan cheese, and red chili flakes. Pour the mixture into a greased baking dish and add the vegetables; mix to distribute. Bake for 20 minutes. Remove and serve warm.

Nutrition Info:

- Per Serving: Calories: 115;Fat: 4g;Protein: 17g;Carbs: 6g.

Soups & Stews

One-pot Chunky Beef Stew

Servings: 6
Cooking Time: 35 Minutes

Ingredients:

- 2 tbsp extra-virgin olive oil
- 1 ½ lb sirloin steak, cubed
- 3 chopped sweet potatoes
- 4 baby carrots, sliced
- 1 celery stalk, sliced
- 1 small onion, chopped
- 4 cups beef broth
- 2 garlic cloves, minced
- 1 cup green peas
- ½ tsp dried thyme
- Sea salt and pepper to taste
- 3 tablespoons arrowroot

Directions:

1. Warm the extra-virgin olive oil in a pot over medium heat. Add the beef, sweet potatoes, baby carrots, celery, garlic, and onion and sauté for 5-8 minutes until the beef is browned. Pour in the broth and thyme. Bring to a boil, lower the heat, and simmer for 15 minutes.
2. Mix the arrowroot with 1 soup ladle in a small bowl and pour the slurry gradually into the pot, whisking continuously. Add the green peas and cook for 2-4 more minutes. Taste and adjust seasoning. Serve warm.

Nutrition Info:

- Per Serving: Calories: 396;Fat: 13g;Protein: 41g;Carbs: 27.6g.

Native Asian Soup With Squash And Shitake

Servings: 2
Cooking Time: 45 Minutes

Ingredients:

- 15 dried shiitake mushrooms, soaked in water
- 6 cups low salt vegetable stock
- ½ butternut squash, peeled and cubed
- 1 tablespoon sesame oil
- 1 onion, quartered and sliced into rings
- 1 large garlic clove, chopped
- 4 stems of pak choy or equivalent
- 1 sprig of thyme or 1 tablespoon dried thyme
- 1 teaspoon tabasco sauce

Directions:

1. Heat sesame on medium-high heat oil in a large pan before sweating the onions and garlic.
2. Add the vegetable stock and bring to a boil over a high heat before adding the squash.
3. Turn down the heat and allow to simmer for 25 to 30 minutes.
4. Soak the mushrooms in the water if not already done, and then press out the liquid and add to the stock into the pot.
5. Use the mushroom water in the stock for extra taste.
6. Except for the greens, add the rest of the ingredients and allow to simmer for 15 minutes more or until the squash is tender.
7. Before serving, add in the chopped greens and let them wilt. Serve with the tabasco sauce if you like it spicy.

Nutrition Info:

- Per Serving: Calories: 1191 ;Fat: 56g ;Protein: 19g ;Carbs: 158g .

Winterrific Soup With Chicken And Dumpling

Servings: 4
Cooking Time: 40 Minutes

Ingredients:

- 2 tablespoons avocado oil
- 1 medium onion, diced
- 3 ribs celery, diced
- 3 small radishes, diced
- 1 small carrot, sliced
- 4 cloves garlic, minced
- 1 pound boneless, skinless chicken thighs
- 1 bay leaf
- 3 sprigs oregano, fresh
- 4 cups bone broth
- 1 teaspoon Himalayan salt, fine
- 1 teaspoon black pepper, ground
- Dumplings:
- 2 large eggs
- 2 tablespoons coconut oil or melted unsalted butter
- 3 tablespoons coconut flour
- Pinch of fine Himalayan salt
- Pinch of ground nutmeg

Directions:

1. Heat a 5-quart pot over medium heat. Pour in the avocado oil and add the onions, celery, radishes, carrots, and garlic. Sauté while stirring often for 8 minutes until the onions are aromatic and translucent.

2. Push the sofrito to the side and place the chicken thighs flat on the bottom of the pot with the bay leaf and the oregano sprigs on top. For 3 minutes, brown on each side then mix the chicken thighs well with the sofrito and pour in the broth. Stir in the salt and pepper. Bring the soup to a boil and cook for 20 minutes.

3. Make the dumplings while the soup cooks. Whisk in a medium-sized bowl together with the eggs and coconut oil. Add the coconut flour, salt, and nutmeg and mix until a dry dough form. Shape into eight equal-sized balls.

4. Reduce the heat to low and stir the soup, bringing it down to a simmer. To gently tear apart the chicken thighs use tongs.

5. Carefully add the dumplings to the soup one at a time. Simmer for about 5 minutes, turning them over with tongs once. When they begin to puff up a little they are done.

6. Remove the soup from the heat and serve right away.

7. Store the soup in an airtight container in the refrigerator for up to 6 days. Bring to a simmer on the stovetop to reheat.

Nutrition Info:

- Per Serving: Calories: 430 ;Fat: 20g ;Protein: 48g ;Carbs: 13g .

Chicken & Ginger Soup

Servings: 4
Cooking Time: 20 Minutes

Ingredients:

- 2 cups skinless leftover roasted chicken, diced
- 4 cups no-salt-added chicken broth
- 1 carrot, chopped
- 2 tbsp extra-virgin olive oil
- 1 onion, chopped
- 1 red bell pepper, chopped
- 1 tbsp grated fresh ginger
- Sea salt and pepper to taste

Directions:

1. Warm the olive oil in a pot over medium heat and add the onion, red bell peppers, carrot, and ginger. Sauté for 5 minutes until the veggies are soft. Mix in chicken, chicken broth, salt, and pepper. Bring to a boil, reduce the heat, and simmer for 5 minutes. Serve immediately.

Nutrition Info:

- Per Serving: Calories: 340;Fat: 16g;Protein: 7g;Carbs: 12g.

Rosemary White Bean Soup

Servings: 4
Cooking Time: 30 Minutes

Ingredients:

- 2 tsp olive oil
- 1 carrot, chopped
- 1 onion, chopped
- 2 garlic cloves, minced
- 1 tbsp rosemary, chopped
- 2 tbsp apple cider vinegar
- 1 cup dried white beans
- ¼ tsp sea salt
- 2 tbsp nutritional yeast

Directions:

1. Heat the oil in a pot over medium heat. Place carrots, onion, and garlic and cook for 5 minutes. Pour in vinegar to deglaze the pot. Stir in 5 cups water and beans and bring to a boil. Lower the heat and simmer for 45 minutes until the beans are soft. Add in salt and nutritional yeast and stir. Serve topped with chopped rosemary.

Nutrition Info:

- Per Serving: Calories: 225;Fat: 3g;Protein: 14g;Carbs: 37g.

Soulful Roasted Vegetable Soup

Servings: 2
Cooking Time: 30 Minutes

Ingredients:

- 2 medium carrots, peeled
- 1 cup baby Brussels sprouts
- 1 rib celery
- ¼ medium head cabbage
- 2 teaspoons fine Himalayan salt, divided
- 2 tablespoons coconut oil
- 2 cups bone broth
- ½ medium Hass avocado, peeled, pitted, and sliced
- 1 green onion, minced
- 4 sprigs fresh cilantro, minced

Directions:

1. Preheat the oven to 400°F.
2. Cut all of the vegetables into small pieces and spread them out on a sheet pan. Sprinkle with 1 teaspoon of the salt and toss with the coconut oil. For 30 minutes, roast.
3. Heat the broth in a saucepan while the vegetables are roasting over medium heat.
4. Divide the vegetables between two serving bowls when they are ready. Add the avocado, green onion, and cilantro, and sprinkle in the remaining teaspoon of salt. Divide the broth between the bowls.
5. Serve immediately. Store leftovers in an airtight container in the fridge for up to 4 days.

Nutrition Info:

- Per Serving: Calories: 276 ;Fat: 23g ;Protein: 6g;Carbs: 19g .s

Cold Vegetable Soup

Servings: 4
Cooking Time: 15 Minutes

Ingredients:

- 2 lb tomatoes, chopped
- 1 peeled cucumber, diced
- 1 red bell pepper, diced
- 1 cup cold water
- 1 slice whole-wheat bread
- 4 green onions, chopped
- 2 garlic cloves, minced
- 2 tbsp extra-virgin olive oil
- 2 tbsp white wine vinegar
- Sea salt to taste

Directions:

1. Place half of the tomatoes, cucumber, bell pepper, water, bread, green onions, and garlic in a food processor. Blitz until smooth. Pour in oil, salt, and vinegar and pulse until combined. Transfer to a bowl and combine with remaining tomatoes. Let chill in the fridge for 1-2 hours.

Nutrition Info:

- Per Serving: Calories: 155;Fat: 8g;Protein: 3g;Carbs: 20g.

Rice Noodle Soup With Beans

Servings: 6
Cooking Time: 10 Minutes

Ingredients:

- 2 carrots, chopped
- 2 celery stalks, chopped
- 6 cups vegetable broth
- 8 oz brown rice noodles
- 1 can pinto beans
- 1 tsp dried thyme

Directions:

1. Place a pot over medium heat and add in the carrots, celery, and vegetable broth. Bring to a boil. Add in noodles, beans, dried thyme, salt, and pepper. Reduce the heat and simmer for 5 minutes. Serve and enjoy!

Nutrition Info:

- Per Serving: Calories: 210;Fat: 1g;Protein: 6g;Carbs: 45g.

Green Bean & Zucchini Velouté

Servings: 6
Cooking Time: 30 Minutes

Ingredients:

- 2 tbsp minced jarred pimiento
- 3 tbsp extra-virgin olive oil
- 1 onion, chopped
- 1 garlic clove, minced
- 2 cups green beans
- 4 cups vegetable broth
- 3 medium zucchini, sliced
- ½ tsp dried marjoram
- ½ cup plain almond milk

Directions:

1. Heat oil in a pot and sauté onion and garlic for 5 minutes. Add in green beans and broth. Cook for 10 minutes. Stir in zucchini and cook for 10 minutes. Transfer to a food processor and pulse until smooth. Return to the pot and mix in almond milk; cook until hot. Top with pimiento.

Nutrition Info:

- Per Serving: Calories: 95;Fat: 7g;Protein: 2g;Carbs: 8g.

Turmeric Cauliflower Soup

Servings: 4
Cooking Time: 35 Minutes

Ingredients:

- 1 cauliflower head, chopped
- ½ tsp turmeric powder
- 1 sweet potato, diced
- 1 onion, diced
- 1 carrot, diced
- 1 cup coconut milk
- 3 cups vegetable broth
- 2 tbsp coconut oil

Directions:

1. Melt the coconut oil in your Instant Pot on "Sauté". Add the onion and carrots and sauté for 3 minutes. Add the rest of the ingredients. Season with salt and pepper. Stir to combine well. Close the lid, choose the "Manual", and cook at high pressure for 15 minutes. Once cooking is complete, press Cancel and allow for a natural pressure release for 10 minutes. Release any remaining steam before opening the lid. Blend with a hand blender until smooth. Transfer to a serving bowl and enjoy.

Nutrition Info:

- Per Serving: Calories: 115;Fat: 3g;Protein: 3g;Carbs: 20g.

Green Bean & Rice Soup

Servings: 4
Cooking Time: 50 Minutes

Ingredients:

- 2 tbsp extra-virgin olive oil
- 1 medium onion, minced
- 2 garlic cloves minced
- ½ cup brown rice
- 1 cup green beans, chopped
- 2 tbsp chopped parsley

Directions:

1. Heat oil in a pot over medium heat. Place in onion and garlic and sauté for 3 minutes. Add in rice, 4 cups water, salt, and pepper. Bring to a boil, lower the heat, and simmer for 15 minutes. Stir in beans and cook for 10 minutes. Top with parsley. Serve and enjoy!

Nutrition Info:

- Per Serving: Calories: 170;Fat: 8g;Protein: 1g;Carbs: 23g.

Cayenne Pumpkin Soup

Servings: 6
Cooking Time: 55 Minutes

Ingredients:

- 1 pumpkin, sliced
- 3 tbsp extra-virgin olive oil
- 1 tsp sea salt
- 2 red bell peppers
- 1 onion, halved
- 1 head garlic
- ¼ tsp cayenne pepper
- ½ tsp ground coriander
- ½ tsp ground cumin
- Toasted pumpkin seeds

Directions:

1. Preheat your oven to 350ºF. Brush the pumpkin slices with oil and sprinkle with salt. Arrange them skin-side-down and on a greased baking dish; bake for 20 minutes. Brush the onion with oil. Cut the top of the garlic head and brush with oil. Add the bell peppers, onion, and garlic to the pumpkin. Bake for 10 minutes. Cool.

2. Take out the flesh from the pumpkin skin and transfer to a food processor. Cut the pepper roughly, peel and cut the onion, and remove the cloves from the garlic head. Transfer to the food processor and pour in 6 cups of water. Blend the soup until smooth. If it's very thick, add a bit of water to reach your desired consistency. Sprinkle with salt, cayenne pepper, coriander, and cumin. Serve.

Nutrition Info:

- Per Serving: Calories: 130;Fat: 8g;Protein: 1g;Carbs: 16g.

Brussels Sprouts & Tofu Soup

Servings: 4
Cooking Time: 40 Minutes

Ingredients:

- 7 oz firm tofu, cubed
- 2 tsp olive oil
- 1 cup sliced mushrooms
- 1 lb Brussels sprouts, halved
- 1 garlic clove, minced
- ½-inch piece minced ginger
- Sea salt to taste
- 2 tbsp apple cider vinegar
- 2 tsp low-sodium soy sauce
- 1 tsp pure date sugar
- ¼ tsp red pepper flakes
- 1 scallion, chopped

Directions:

1. Heat the oil in a skillet over medium heat. Place mushrooms, Brussels sprouts, garlic, ginger, and salt. Sauté for 7-8 minutes until the veggies are soft. Pour in 4 cups of water, vinegar, soy sauce, sugar, pepper flakes, and tofu. Bring to a boil, then lower the heat and simmer for 5-10 minutes. Top with scallions and serve.

Nutrition Info:

- Per Serving: Calories: 135;Fat: 8g;Protein: 9g;Carbs: 8g.

Vegetable Chili

Servings: 4
Cooking Time: 30 Minutes

Ingredients:

- 1 onion, chopped
- 1 cup vegetable broth
- 2 garlic cloves, minced
- 1 turnip, cubed
- 1 carrot, chopped
- 2 tsp olive oil
- 1 can tomatoes
- 1 tbsp tomato paste
- 1 can chickpeas
- 1 tsp chili powder
- Sea salt and pepper to taste
- ¼ cup parsley, chopped

Directions:

1. Heat oil in a pot over medium heat. Place in onion and garlic and sauté for 3 minutes. Add in turnip, carrot, tomatoes, broth, tomato paste, chickpeas, and chili; season. Simmer for 20 minutes. Top with parsley. Serve.

Nutrition Info:

- Per Serving: Calories: 180;Fat: 5g;Protein: 7g;Carbs: 30g.

Power Green Soup

Servings: 4
Cooking Time: 45 Minutes

Ingredients:

- 1 tbsp cilantro, chopped
- 2 cups coconut milk
- 4 cups kale, chopped
- 4 cups spinach, chopped
- 1 lb collard greens chopped
- Sea salt to taste

Directions:

1. Mix the coconut milk and 2 cups of water in a large pot over medium heat, then sprinkle with salt. Bring to a boil. Reduce the heat, add the greens and cook for 10 minutes or until wilted. Pour the soup in a blender, then pulse until creamy and smooth. Serve immediately.

Nutrition Info:

- Per Serving: Calories: 335;Fat: 30g;Protein: 6g;Carbs: 18g.

Mediterranean Stew With Lentil And Broccoli

Servings: 4

Cooking Time: 30 Minutes

Ingredients:

- 1 tablespoon extra-virgin olive oil, plus additional for drizzling
- 1 small onion, finely chopped
- 1 small carrot, chopped
- 2 cloves garlic, minced
- 2 cups vegetable broth
- 1 cup dried green or brown lentils
- 1 teaspoon oregano, dried
- 6 cups broccoli florets
- 1 teaspoon salt
- ¼ teaspoon black pepper, freshly ground
- ½ cup pitted green olives, sliced
- ¼ cup fresh Italian parsley, chopped

Directions:

1. Heat the olive oil in a large pot over high heat.
2. Add the onion, carrot, and garlic. Sauté for 5 minutes.
3. Add the vegetable broth, lentils, and oregano and bring to a boil. Reduce the heat to simmer. For 15 to 20 minutes, cook the soup until the lentils are tender.
4. Add the broccoli, cover the pot, and simmer for 5 minutes more.
5. Remove the pot from the heat and stir in the olives and parsley. Stir in some water if the soup is too thick.
6. Ladle the soup into bowls, drizzle with a little olive oil, and serve.

Nutrition Info:

- Per Serving: Calories: 182 ;Fat: 6g ;Protein: 11g ;Carbs: 24g .

Poultry And Meats

Chicken Stir-fry With Bell Pepper

Servings: 4
Cooking Time: 30 Minutes

Ingredients:

- 3 tbsp avocado oil
- ½ tsp red pepper flakes
- 1 red bell pepper, chopped
- 1 onion, chopped
- 1 ½ lb chicken breasts, cubed
- 2 garlic cloves, minced
- Sea salt and pepper to taste

Directions:

1. Warm the avocado oil in a skillet over medium heat and place in bell pepper, onion, and chicken. Sauté for 10 minutes. Stir in garlic, salt, and pepper and cook for another 30 seconds. Sprinkle with red flakes and serve.

Nutrition Info:

- Per Serving: Calories: 180;Fat: 14g;Protein: 2g;Carbs: 7g.

Magnificent Herbaceous Pork Meatballs

Servings: 2
Cooking Time: 20 Minutes

Ingredients:

- 8 ounces lean pork, minced
- 1 garlic clove, crushed
- ¼ cup bread, 100% wholegrain crumbs
- 1 teaspoon thyme, dried
- 1 teaspoon basil, dried
- 2 tablespoons extra virgin olive oil
- 1 cup spaghetti, 100% wholegrain or gluten-free
- Sauce:
- 1 tablespoon extra-virgin olive oil
- 1 red onion, finely chopped
- 1 can tomatoes, chopped
- 1 red pepper, finely chopped
- ½ cup water
- 1 tablespoon fresh basil

Directions:

1. In a bowl, mix the pork mince, 1 tablespoon oil, garlic, breadcrumbs, and herbs. Season with a little black pepper and separate into 8 balls, rolling with the palms of your hands.
2. In a pan over medium heat, heat 1 tablespoon oil and add onions and peppers, sauté for a few minutes until soft.
3. Add the tomatoes and ½ cup water.
4. For 15 minutes, cover and lower heat to simmer.
5. Boil your water and cook spaghetti to recommended guidelines.
6. Heat 1 tablespoon oil and add the meatballs to a separate pan, turning carefully to brown the surface of each. Continue this for 5 to 7 minutes before adding to the sauce and simmering for 5 minutes more.
7. Drain spaghetti, portion up, and pour a generous portion of meatballs and sauce over the top to serve.
8. Sprinkle with a little freshly torn basil.

Nutrition Info:

- Per Serving: Calories: 435 ;Fat: 23g ;Protein: 37g ;Carbs: 19g .

Lemon & Caper Turkey Scaloppine

Servings: 4
Cooking Time: 25 Minutes

Ingredients:

- 1 tbsp capers
- ¼ cup whole-wheat flour
- Sea salt and pepper to taste
- 4 turkey breast cutlets
- 2 tbsp olive oil
- 3 lemons, juiced
- 1 lemon, zested
- 1 tbsp chopped parsley

Directions:

1. Pound the turkey with a rolling pin to ¼-inch thickness. Combine flour, salt, and pepper in a bowl. Roll each cutlet piece in the flour, shaking off the excess. Warm the olive oil in a skillet over medium heat. Sear the cutlets for 4 minutes on both sides. Transfer to a plate and cover with aluminium foil. Pour the lemon juice and lemon zest in the skillet to scrape up the browned bits that stick to the bottom of the skillet. Stir in capers and rosemary. Cook for 2 minutes until the sauce has thickened slightly. Drizzle the sauce over the cutlets. Serve.

Nutrition Info:

- Per Serving: Calories: 190;Fat: 14g;Protein: 2g;Carbs: 9g.

Herby Green Whole Chicken

Servings: 6
Cooking Time: 1 Hour 45 Minutes

Ingredients:

- 1 sweet onion, quartered
- 1 whole chicken
- 2 lemons, halved
- 4 garlic cloves, crushed
- 4 fresh thyme sprigs
- 4 fresh rosemary sprigs
- 4 fresh parsley sprigs
- 3 bay leaves
- 2 tbsp olive oil
- Sea salt and pepper to taste

Directions:

1. Preheat your oven to 400ºF. Put the chicken in a greased pan. Stuff it with lemons, onion, garlic, thyme, rosemary, parsley, and bay leaves into the cavity. Brush the chicken with olive oil, and season lightly with sea salt and pepper. Roast the chicken for about 1 ½ hours until golden brown and cooked through. Remove the chicken from the oven and let it sit for 10 minutes. Remove the lemons, onion, and herbs from the cavity and serve.

Nutrition Info:

- Per Serving: Calories: 260;Fat: 9g;Protein: 39g;Carbs: 6g.

Apple-glazed Whole Chicken

Servings: 4
Cooking Time: 60 Minutes

Ingredients:

- 1 whole chicken, cut into 8 pieces
- 1 cup sugar-free apple juice
- 1 tbsp brown rice flour
- Sea salt and pepper to taste
- ½ tsp ground cinnamon
- 1 tsp ground cumin
- 2 tsp sweet paprika
- ½ tsp garlic powder

Directions:

1. Preheat your oven to 375ºF. Place the chicken pieces in a baking pan. In a small bowl, combine the brown rice flour, salt, ground cinnamon, cumin, paprika, garlic powder, and pepper. Rub the spice mix onto the chicken pieces. Carefully pour the apple juice into the pan. Place the pan in the oven and bake for 35-45 minutes, or until the chicken is golden brown and cooked through. Serve.

Nutrition Info:

- Per Serving: Calories: 370;Fat: 20g;Protein: 38g;Carbs: 10g.

Italian Turkey Meatballs

Servings: 4
Cooking Time: 7 Hours 15 Minutes

Ingredients:

- 1 spaghetti squash, halved lengthwise, scoop out seeds
- 1 can diced tomatoes
- ½ tsp garlic powder
- ½ tsp dried oregano
- ½ tsp sea salt
- 1 large egg, whisked
- ½ white onion, minced
- 1 lb ground turkey
- Sea salt and pepper to taste
- ½ tsp dried basil
- 1 cup arugula

Directions:

1. Pour the diced tomatoes into your slow cooker. Sprinkle with garlic powder, oregano, and salt. Put in the squash halves, cut-side down. In a medium bowl, mix together the turkey, egg, onion, salt, pepper, and basil. Shape the turkey mixture into balls and place them in the slow cooker around the spaghetti squash. Cover the cooker and set to "Low". Cook for 7 hours. Transfer the squash to a work surface and use a fork to shred it into spaghetti-like strands. Combine the strands with the tomato sauce, top with the meatballs and arugula, and serve.

Nutrition Info:

- Per Serving: Calories: 250;Fat: 8g;Protein: 23g;Carbs: 21g.

Appetizing And Healthy Turkey Gumbo

Servings: 1
Cooking Time: 2 Hours

Ingredients:

- 1 whole turkey
- 1 onion, quartered
- stalk of celery, chopped
- 3 cloves garlic, chopped
- ½ cup okra
- 1 can tomatoes, chopped
- 1 tablespoon extra-virgin olive oil
- 1-2 bay leaves
- black pepper

Directions:

1. Take the first four ingredients and add 2 cups of water in a stockpot then heat on a high heat until boiling.
2. Lower the heat and simmer for 45 to 50 minutes or until turkey is cooked through.
3. Remove the turkey and strain the broth.
4. Grab a skillet and heat the oil on a medium heat and brown the rest of the vegetables for 5 to 10 minutes.
5. Stir until tender and then add to the broth.
6. Add the tomatoes and turkey meat to the broth and stir.
7. Add the bay leaves and continue to cook for an hour or until the sauce has thickened.
8. Season with black pepper and enjoy.

Nutrition Info:

- Per Serving: Calories: 179 ;Fat: 7g ;Protein: 5g ;Carbs: 28g .

Gingered Beef Stir-fry With Peppers

Servings: 4
Cooking Time: 15 Minutes

Ingredients:

- 2 tbsp olive oil
- 1 lb ground beef
- 2 green garlic stalks, minced
- 6 scallions, chopped
- 2 red bell peppers, chopped
- 2 tbsp grated fresh ginger
- ½ tsp sea salt
- 2 tbsp tarragon, chopped

Directions:

1. Warm the olive oil in a skillet over medium heat and place the ground beef. Cook for 5 minutes until browns. Stir in scallions, green garlic, bell peppers, ginger, and salt and cook for 4 more minutes until the bell peppers are soft. Top with tarragon and serve immediately.

Nutrition Info:

- Per Serving: Calories: 600;Fat: 20g;Protein: 2g;Carbs: 10g.

Nut Free Turkey Burgers With Ginger

Servings: 4
Cooking Time: 10 Minutes

Ingredients:

- 1½ pounds turkey, ground
- 1 large egg, lightly beaten
- 2 tablespoons coconut flour
- ½ cup onion, finely chopped
- 1 garlic clove, minced
- 2 teaspoons fresh ginger root, minced
- 1 tablespoon cilantro, fresh
- 1 teaspoon salt
- ¼ teaspoon black pepper, freshly ground
- 1 tablespoon extra-virgin olive oil

Directions:

1. Combine in a medium bowl the ground turkey, egg, flour, onion, garlic, ginger root, cilantro, salt, and pepper and mix well.
2. Form the turkey mixture into four patties.
3. Heat the olive oil in a large skillet over medium-high heat.
4. Cook the burgers and flip it once until firm for 3 to 4 minutes on each side. Serve.

Nutrition Info:

- Per Serving: Calories: 320 ;Fat: 20g ;Protein: 34g ;Carbs: 2g .

Traditional Beef Bolognese

Servings: 4
Cooking Time: 8 Hours 15 Minutes

Ingredients:

- 3 garlic cloves, minced
- 1 tbsp extra-virgin olive oil
- 1 chopped onion
- 1 chopped celery stalk
- 1 chopped carrot
- 1 lb ground beef
- 1 can diced tomatoes
- 1 tbsp white wine vinegar
- ⅛ tsp ground nutmeg
- ½ cup red wine
- ½ tsp red pepper flakes
- Sea salt and pepper to taste

Directions:

1. Grease your slow cooker with olive oil. Add onion, garlic, celery, carrot, ground beef, tomatoes, vinegar, nutmeg, wine, pepper flakes, salt, and pepper. Using a fork, break up the ground beef as much as possible. Cover the cooker and cook for 8 hours on "Low". Serve and enjoy!

Nutrition Info:

- Per Serving: Calories: 315;Fat: 20g;Protein: 21g;Carbs: 10g.

Cumin Lamb Meatballs With Aioli

Servings: 4

Cooking Time: 30 Minutes

Ingredients:

- 1 tsp ground cumin
- 2 tbsp chopped cilantro
- 1 ½ lb ground lamb
- 1 tbsp dried oregano
- 1 tsp onion powder
- 1 tsp garlic powder
- Sea salt and pepper to taste
- ½ cup garlic aioli

Directions:

1. Preheat your oven to 400°F. Combine the ground lamb, cumin, cilantro, rosemary, oregano, onion powder, garlic powder, salt, and pepper in a bowl. Shape 20 meatballs out of the mixture and transfer to a parchment-lined baking sheet. Bake for 15 minutes until the meat reaches an internal temperature of 140°F. Serve warm with aioli.

Nutrition Info:

- Per Serving: Calories: 450;Fat: 24g;Protein: 2g;Carbs: 11g.

Veggie & Beef Brisket

Servings: 4

Cooking Time: 60 Minutes

Ingredients:

- 4 beef tenderloin fillets
- 4 sweet potatoes, chopped
- 1 onion, chopped
- 2 bay leaves
- 2 tbsp olive oil
- 2 cups chopped carrots
- 3 tbsp chopped garlic
- 3 tbsp Worcestershire sauce
- 2 celery stalks, chopped
- Black pepper to taste
- 1 tbsp Knorr demi-glace sauce

Directions:

1. Heat 1 tbsp oil in your pressure cooker on "Sauté". Sauté the onion until caramelized. Transfer to a bowl. Season the meat with pepper to taste. Heat the remaining oil and cook the meat until browned on all sides. Add the remaining ingredients and 2 cups of water. Close the lid and cook for 30 minutes on "Manual" on High pressure. When cooking is complete, release the pressure naturally for 10 minutes. Transfer the meat and veggies to a serving platter. Whisk the Knorr Demi-Glace sauce in the pot and simmer for 5 minutes until thickened on "Sauté". Pour the gravy over the meat and enjoy.

Nutrition Info:

- Per Serving: Calories: 400;Fat: 20g;Protein: 28g;Carbs: 10g.

Tastylicious Chicken Cajun With Prawn

Servings: 2

Cooking Time: 35 Minutes

Ingredients:

- 2 free range chicken breasts, chopped and skinless
- 1 onion, chopped
- 1 red pepper, chopped
- 2 garlic cloves, crushed
- 10 king prawns, fresh or frozen
- 1 teaspoon cayenne pepper
- 1 teaspoon chili powder
- 1 teaspoon paprika
- ¼ teaspoon chili powder
- 1 teaspoon oregano, dried
- 1 teaspoon thyme, dried
- 1 cup rice, brown or wholegrain
- 1 tablespoon extra-virgin olive oil
- 1 can tomatoes, chopped
- 2 cups homemade chicken stock

Directions:

1. Mix the spices and herbs in a separate bowl to form your Cajun spice mix.
2. Grab a large pan and add the olive oil, heating on medium heat.
3. Add the chicken and brown each side for around 4 to 5 minutes then place to one side.
4. Add the onion to the pan and fry until soft.
5. Add the garlic, prawns, Cajun seasoning, and red pepper to the pan and cook for 5 minutes or until prawns become opaque.
6. Add the brown rice along with the chopped tomatoes, chicken, and chicken stock to the pan.
7. Cover the pan and allow to simmer for 25 minutes or until the rice is soft.

Nutrition Info:

- Per Serving: Calories: 173 ;Fat: 7g ;Protein: 8g ;Carbs: 21g .

Homemade Chicken & Pepper Cacciatore

Servings: 4

Cooking Time: 30 Minutes

Ingredients:

- 1 ½ lb chicken breasts, cubed
- 3 mixed peppers, cut into strips
- 28 oz canned diced tomatoes
- ½ cup chopped black olives
- 2 tbsp extra-virgin olive oil
- 1 tsp onion powder
- 1 tsp garlic powder
- Sea salt and pepper to taste

Directions:

1. Warm the olive oil in a large saucepan over medium heat. Add the chicken and sauté for 8-10 minutes until evenly browned, stirring occasionally. Add the peppers, tomatoes, olives, onion powder, garlic powder, salt, and pepper and allow to simmer for 10 minutes, stirring occasionally, or until the chicken is cooked through.

Nutrition Info:

- Per Serving: Calories: 305;Fat: 11g;Protein: 18g;Carbs: 34g.

Sweet Balsamic Chicken

Servings: 4
Cooking Time: 30 Minutes

Ingredients:

- 1 shallot, minced
- 1 tsp sea salt
- 2 tbsp honey
- ¼ cup balsamic vinegar
- 4 chicken breasts

Directions:

1. Preheat your oven to 350°F. Mix the shallot, salt, honey, and vinegar in a baking dish until the honey dissolves. Add in chicken breast and toss to coat and bake for 20 minutes. Let rest for 5 minutes and serve.

Nutrition Info:

- Per Serving: Calories: 232;Fat: 5g;Protein: 35g;Carbs: 13g.

Korean Vegetable Salad With Smoky Crispy Kalua Pork

Servings: 6
Cooking Time: 10 Hours And 10 Minutes

Ingredients:

- Kalua Pork:
- 3 pounds bone-in pork shoulder
- 1 tablespoon Himalayan salt, fine
- 2 tablespoons liquid smoke
- 1 sweet onion, quartered
- 1 cup water
- 1 banana peel
- Vegetable Salad:
- 4 cups water
- 4 cups chopped watercress, ong choy, or broccoli florets
- 1 tablespoon garlic, minced
- 1 teaspoon fresh ginger, peeled and minced
- 1 tablespoon coconut aminos
- 1 tablespoon coconut vinegar
- 1 tablespoon sesame oil
- 1 teaspoon Himalayan salt, fine
- 1 teaspoon black pepper, ground

Directions:

1. On a flat surface, pat the pork shoulder dry and stand it up with the layer of fat facing up. Score the fat with a very sharp knife, gently cut the slits into a diagonal pattern.

2. Sprinkle the salt all over the pork shoulder, then rub in the liquid smoke until the pork is well covered.

3. In the slow cooker, place the onion quarters. Add the water and banana peel. Place the pork shoulder fat side up on top of the onions. Cook on low for 9 to 10 hours.

4. Transfer the pork to a large bowl when it's done. Remove the bone and use two forks to shred the meat. Spoon 2 to 3 tablespoons of the liquid from the slow cooker onto the shredded pork.

5. Crisp up the shredded pork. Heat a large cast-iron skillet over medium heat. Add the shredded pork in one even layer when it's hot. Let it cook undisturbed for 5 minutes. Stir well, flatten again, and cook undisturbed for 5 minutes more. Then scrape it up from the bottom of the skillet using a spatula and stir.

6. Blanch the vegetables for the salad while the pork is crisping. Bring the water to a simmer in a large pot over medium heat. Add the watercress, garlic, and ginger, cover, and cook for 3 minutes. Prepare a large bowl of ice water. Remove the vegetables from the steaming water and quickly place in the ice bath for 2 to 3 minutes. Drain and pat dry.

7. Place the coconut aminos, vinegar, sesame oil, salt, and pepper in a small bowl. Add the blanched vegetables and gently toss to combine. Serve the crispy pork with this delicious cold salad.

8. Store the pork in an airtight container in the fridge for up to 5 days. Store the salad in a separate airtight container in the fridge for no more than 2 days.

Nutrition Info:

- Per Serving: Calories: 536 ;Fat: 36g ;Protein: 44g;Carbs: 6g .

Fish And Seafood

Hawaiian Tuna

Servings: 4

Cooking Time: 35 Minutes

Ingredients:

- 2 lb tuna, cubed
- 1 cup pineapple chunks
- ¼ cup chopped cilantro
- 2 tbsp chopped parsley
- 2 garlic cloves, minced
- 1 tbsp coconut oil
- 1 tbsp coconut aminos
- Sea salt and pepper to taste

Directions:

1. Preheat your oven to 400ºF. Add the tuna, pineapple, cilantro, parsley, garlic, coconut aminos, salt, and pepper to a baking dish and stir to coat. Bake for 15-20 minutes, or until the fish feels firm to the touch. Serve warm.

Nutrition Info:

- Per Serving: Calories: 410;Fat: 15g;Protein: 59g;Carbs: 7g.

Wonderful Baked Sea Bass With Tomatoes, Olives, And Capers

Servings: 4

Cooking Time: 15 Minutes

Ingredients:

- 2 tablespoons extra-virgin olive oil
- 4 sea bass fillets, 5 ounces
- 1 small onion, diced
- ½ cup vegetable or chicken broth
- 1 cup diced tomatoes, canned
- ½ cup Kalamata olives, pitted and chopped
- 2 tablespoons capers, drained
- 2 cups spinach, packed
- 1 teaspoon salt
- ¼ teaspoon black pepper, freshly ground

Directions:

1. Preheat the oven to 375ºF.
2. Add the olive oil in a baking dish. Place the fish fillets in the dish, turning to coat both sides with the oil.
3. Top the fish with the onion, vegetable broth, tomatoes, olives, capers, spinach, salt, and pepper.
4. Cover the baking dish with aluminum foil and place it in the preheated oven. Bake for 15 minutes, or until the fish is cooked through.

Nutrition Info:

- Per Serving: Calories: 273 ;Fat: 12g ;Protein: 35g ;Carbs: 5g .

Grilled Adobo Shrimp Skewers

Servings: 4
Cooking Time: 40 Minutes + Chilling Time

Ingredients:

- 1 ½ lb shrimp, peeled and deveined, tails on
- ½ cup olive oil
- ¼ cup lime juice
- 2 tbsp chipotles in adobo
- 1 tbsp honey
- ½ tsp onion powder
- 2 garlic cloves, minced
- 2 tsp hot sauce
- 2 tsp cayenne pepper
- 1 tsp ground coriander
- Sea salt and pepper to taste

Directions:

1. Add the olive oil, lime juice, chipotles in adobo, honey, onion powder, garlic, hot sauce, chile powder, ground coriander, salt, and pepper to your or food processor. Puree until smooth. Put the shrimp and marinade in a sealable bag; shake to coat well. Refrigerate for 3 hours.

2. Heat your grill to high. Thread the marinated shrimp onto bamboo skewers and grill them for 2-3 minutes per side until opaque. Serve warm.

Nutrition Info:

- Per Serving: Calories: 440;Fat: 30g;Protein: 34g;Carbs: 9g.

Crispy Pan-seared Salmon

Servings: 4
Cooking Time: 30 Minutes

Ingredients:

- 6 cups chopped mustard greens
- ¼ cup olive oil
- 4 salmon fillets
- Sea salt and pepper to taste
- 1 lemon, zested and juiced
- 3 garlic cloves, minced

Directions:

1. Warm 2 tbsp of olive oil in a skillet over medium heat. Sprinkle salmon fillets with salt, pepper, and lemon zest. Place them in the skillet, skin-side up, and sear until golden-brown on the bottom. Turn and cook for another 3-4 minutes until crispy. Set aside covered with foil.

2. Warm the remaining olive oil in the skillet, add the mustard greens, and cook for 7 minutes until soft. Stir in garlic and cook for another 30 seconds. Mix in lemon juice, salt, and pepper and cook for 2 more minutes. Remove to a serving plate and top with salmon. Enjoy!

Nutrition Info:

- Per Serving: Calories: 370;Fat: 26g;Protein: 1g;Carbs: 4g.

Tasty Sardine Donburi

Servings: 4 To 6
Cooking Time: 45 To 50 Minutes

Ingredients:

- 2 cups brown rice, rinsed well
- 4 cups water
- ½ teaspoon salt
- Three 4 ounces cans sardines packed in water, drained
- 3 scallions, sliced thin
- 1 inch piece fresh ginger, grated
- 4 tablespoons sesame oil, or extra-virgin olive oil, divided

Directions:

1. Combine the rice, water, and salt in a large pot. Bring to a boil over high heat. Reduce the heat to low. Cover and cook for 45 to 50 minutes until tender.
2. Roughly mash the sardines in a medium bowl.
3. Add the sardines, scallions, and ginger to the pot when the rice is done. Mix thoroughly.
4. Divide the rice among four bowls. Drizzle each bowl with 1 teaspoon to 1 tablespoon of sesame oil.

Nutrition Info:

- Per Serving: Calories: 604 ;Fat: 24g ;Protein: 25g ;Carbs: 74g .

Hazelnut Crusted Trout Fillets

Servings: 4
Cooking Time: 30 Minutes

Ingredients:

- 4 boneless trout fillets
- 1 cup hazelnuts, ground
- 1 tbsp coconut oil, melted
- 2 tbsp chopped thyme
- Sea salt and pepper to taste
- Lemon wedges, for garnish

Directions:

1. Preheat your oven to 375ºF. Place the trout fillets on a greased baking sheet skin-side down. Season with salt and pepper. Gently press ¼ cup of ground hazelnuts into the flesh of each fillet. Drizzle the melted coconut oil over the nuts and then sprinkle with thyme. Bake for 15 minutes, or until the fish is cooked through. Serve.

Nutrition Info:

- Per Serving: Calories: 670;Fat: 59g;Protein: 29g;Carbs: 15g.

Appealing Lemon With Wild Salmon And Mixed Vegetables

Servings: 4
Cooking Time: 25 To 30 Minutes

Ingredients:

- Four 5 ounces wild salmon fillets
- 1 teaspoon salt, divided
- 1 lemon, washed and sliced thin
- 1 broccoli head, roughly chopped
- 1 cauliflower head, roughly chopped
- 1 small bunch (4 to 6) carrots, cut into coins

Directions:

1. Preheat the oven to 400°F.
2. Line a baking sheet with parchment paper.
3. Place the salmon on the prepared sheet.
4. Sprinkle the salmon with ½ teaspoon of salt. Drape each fillet with a few lemon slices.
5. Place the sheet in the preheated oven and bake for 15 to 20 minutes, or until the salmon is opaque and flakes easily with a fork.
6. Fill a pot with 3 inches of water and insert a steamer basket while the salmon cooks. Bring to a boil over high heat.
7. Add the broccoli, cauliflower, and carrots to the pot. Cover and cook for 8 to 10 minutes.
8. Sprinkle with the remaining ½ teaspoon of salt.
9. Top each salmon fillet with a heaping pile of vegetables, and serve.

Nutrition Info:

- Per Serving: Calories: 330 ;Fat: 13g ;Protein: 35g ;Carbs: 20g.

Spicy Shrimp Scampi

Servings: 4
Cooking Time: 25 Minutes

Ingredients:

- 1 ½ lb shrimp, peeled and tails removed
- 1 tsp ancho chili powder
- ¼ cup coconut oil
- 1 tsp paprika
- 1 onion, finely chopped
- 1 red bell pepper, chopped
- 2 garlic cloves, minced
- 1 lemon, zested and juiced
- Sea salt and pepper to taste

Directions:

1. Warm the coconut oil in a skillet over medium heat. Add the onion and red bell pepper and cook for 6 minutes until tender. Put in shrimp and cook for 5 minutes until it´s pink. Mix in garlic and cook for another 30 seconds. Add lemon juice, lemon zest, ancho chili powder, paprika, salt, and pepper and simmer for 3 minutes. Serve warm.

Nutrition Info:

- Per Serving: Calories: 350;Fat: 17g;Protein: 1g;Carbs: 11g.

Old Bay Crab Cakes

Servings: 4
Cooking Time: 30 Minutes

Ingredients:

- ½ cup shredded carrots
- 2 scallions, chopped
- 2 lb cooked lump crabmeat
- ½ cup shredded coconut
- ½ cup coconut flour
- 2 eggs
- 1 tsp Old Bay spice mix
- 1 tsp lemon zest
- 2 tbsp olive oil

Directions:

1. Mix together the crab, coconut, coconut flour, carrot, scallions, eggs, Old Bay spice mix, and lemon zest in a large bowl. Shape the mixture into 8 patties and flatten them until they are about 1 inch thick. Warm the olive oil in a skillet over medium heat. Add the crab cakes and sear for about 6 minutes per side until cooked through and golden on both sides, turning once. Serve.

Nutrition Info:

- Per Serving: Calories: 405;Fat: 20g;Protein: 49g;Carbs: 5g.

Lime Salmon Burgers

Servings: 4
Cooking Time: 30 Minutes + Chilling Time

Ingredients:

- 2 tbsp olive oil
- 1 lime, cut into wedges
- 1 tsp garlic powder
- 1 scallion, chopped
- 1 lb cooked salmon fillet, flaked
- 2 eggs
- ¾ cup almond flour
- 1 lime, juiced and zested
- 1 tbsp chopped dill
- A pinch of sea salt

Directions:

1. Combine the salmon, eggs, almond flour, garlic powder, scallion, lime juice, lime zest, dill, and salt in a large bowl and mix until the mixture holds together when pressed. Divide the salmon mixture into 4 equal portions, and press them into patties about ½ inch thick. Refrigerate them for about 30 minutes to firm up.
2. Warm the olive oil in a skillet over medium heat. Add the salmon patties and brown for about 5 minutes per side, turning once. Serve the patties with lime wedges.

Nutrition Info:

- Per Serving: Calories: 245;Fat: 17g;Protein: 19g;Carbs: 5g.

Smoky Boneless Haddock With Pea Risotto

Servings: 2
Cooking Time: 40 Minutes

Ingredients:

- 2 smoked haddock fillets, boneless and skinless
- 1 tablespoon extra-virgin olive oil
- 1 white onion, finely diced
- 2 cups brown rice
- 4 cups vegetable stock
- 1 cup spinach leaves, fresh
- 1 cup peas, frozen
- 3 tablespoons low fat Greek yogurt
- a pinch of black pepper
- 4 lemon wedges
- 1 cup of arugula

Directions:

1. Heat the oil in a large pan on a medium heat.
2. For 5 minutes, sauté the chopped onion until soft before adding in the rice and stirring for 1 to 2 minutes.
3. Add half of the stock and stir slowly.
4. Slowly add the rest of the stock whilst continuously stirring for up to 20 to 30 minutes.
5. Stir in the spinach and peas fish to the risotto.
6. Place the fish on top of the rice, cover and steam for 10 minutes.
7. To break up the fish fillets, use your fork and stir into the rice with the yogurt.
8. Sprinkle with freshly ground pepper to serve and a squeeze of fresh lemon.
9. Garnish with the lemon wedges and serve with the arugula.

Nutrition Info:

- Per Serving: Calories: 4023 ;Fat: 441g ;Protein: 35g ;Carbs: 22 .

Nostalgic Tuna And Avocado Salad Sandwiches

Servings: 4
Cooking Time: 0 Minutes

Ingredients:

- Three 6 ounces cans wild tuna, drained
- 1 large avocado, halved and pitted
- 1 celery stalk, finely chopped
- ½ cup fresh parsley, minced
- 8 slices gluten-free bread, or Quinoa Flatbread

Directions:

1. Roughly mash the tuna in a medium bowl.
2. Into the bowl with the tuna, scoop the avocado flesh and mash together.
3. Stir in the celery and parsley.
4. Divide the tuna salad among 4 bread slices. Top each with a second bread slice and serve.

Nutrition Info:

- Per Serving: Calories: 503 ;Fat: 25g ;Protein: 7g ;Carbs: 31g .

Salmon In Miso-ginger Sauce

Servings: 4
Cooking Time: 30 Minutes

Ingredients:

- 1 sliced scallion
- 4 boneless salmon fillets
- ⅛ tsp red pepper flakes
- 1 tbsp olive oil
- ¼ cup apple cider
- ¼ tsp porcini powder
- ¼ tsp garlic powder
- ¼ cup white miso
- 1 tbsp white rice vinegar
- ⅛ tsp ground ginger

Directions:

1. Whisk olive oil, apple cider, porcini powder, garlic powder, miso, vinegar, and ginger in a bowl. Set aside.
2. Preheat your oven to 375ºF. Arrange the salmon fillets, skin-side down on a greased baking pan. Pour the prepared sauce over the fillets. Bake in the oven for 15-20 minutes, or until the fish flakes easily with a fork. Garnish with scallion and red pepper flakes and serve.

Nutrition Info:

- Per Serving: Calories: 465;Fat: 19g;Protein: 67g;Carbs: 9g.

Dazzling And Smoky Salmon Hash Browns

Servings: 2
Cooking Time: 35 Minutes

Ingredients:

- 1 large sweet potato, peeled and cubed
- 3 tablespoons extra virgin olive oil
- 1 leek, chopped
- 4 teaspoons dill, chopped
- 1 tablespoon orange peel, grated
- 1 pack smoked salmon, sliced

Directions:

1. Preheat the oven to 325°F.
2. Lightly grease with a little olive oil 2 ramekins or circular baking dishes.
3. Heat the rest of the oil in a skillet over medium heat, and sauté the leeks and the potatoes for 5 minutes.
4. Lower the heat and cook for 10 minutes until tender.
5. Transfer to a separate bowl the potatoes and leeks and crush with a fork to form a mash or use a potato masher.
6. Add the dill, orange peel and the salmon and mix well.
7. Fill the ramekins with half the mixture each, patting to compact.
8. Bake for 15 minutes then remove.
9. Serve in the ramekin and season.

Nutrition Info:

- Per Serving: Calories: 192 ;Fat: 9g ;Protein: 3g ;Carbs: 26g ;Sugar: 8g .

Creamy Crabmeat

Servings: 4
Cooking Time: 15 Minutes

Ingredients:

- ¼ cup olive oil
- 1 small red onion, chopped
- 1 lb lump crabmeat
- ½ celery stalk, chopped
- ½ cup plain yogurt
- ¼ cup chicken broth

Directions:

1. Season the crabmeat with some salt and pepper. Heat the oil in your Instant Pot on "Sauté". Add celery and onion and cook for 3 minutes, or until soft. Add the crabmeat and stir in the broth. Seal and lock the lid and set to "Steam" for 5 minutes on high pressure. Once the cooking is complete, do a quick release and carefully open the lid. Stir in the yogurt and serve.

Nutrition Info:

- Per Serving: Calories: 450;Fat: 10g;Protein: 40g;Carbs: 12g.

Greatest Crispy Fish Tacos And Mango Salsa

Servings: 4
Cooking Time: 10 Minutes

Ingredients:

- Mango Salsa:
- 2 mangoes, peeled, pitted, and diced
- ½ small red onion, finely diced
- 1 jalapeño, minced
- 2 tablespoons lime juice, plus more as needed
- 2 tablespoons cilantro, finely chopped
- Kosher salt
- Avocado Crema:
- 2 avocados, halved and pitted
- Kosher salt
- 2 tablespoons mayonnaise or Vegenaise
- 2 tablespoons lime juice, plus more as needed
- 1 pound tilapia fillets or other white-fleshed fish
- Kosher salt
- Freshly ground black pepper
- 2 eggs
- 1 cup Cup4Cup or other gluten-free flour, 140g
- 1 cup Parmigiano-Reggiano, 30g and finely grated
- 4 tablespoons extra-virgin olive oil, 60ml
- 8 corn tortillas, warmed
- ½ head red or green cabbage, cored and finely shredded
- Lime wedges

Directions:

1. To make the avocado crema. First, place the avocado flesh and ¼ teaspoon salt in a medium bowl. Mash using a fork or a pastry blender until very smooth. Stir in the mayonnaise and lime juice. Taste then adds additional salt and lime juice as preferred. Store, with a piece of plastic wrap pressed directly onto the surface, in the refrigerator for up to 2 days.

2. Rinse the tilapia and pat dry. Halve each fillet lengthwise by slicing down the middle seam. Season with salt and pepper. Whisk the eggs in a shallow bowl. In another small bowl, place the flour, Parmigiano-Reggiano, and ½ teaspoon salt and stir to combine. Dip the fish, one piece at a time, into the eggs and coat evenly and allow any excess to drip off into the bowl. Place in the flour mixture and coat both sides evenly by gently tapping off the excess. Arrange the coated fish on a baking sheet in a single layer.

3. Line another baking sheet with paper towels. Warm 2 tablespoons of the olive oil in a large nonstick skillet over medium-high heat. Working in two batches, place the fish pieces in the skillet and cook until golden brown on each side and opaque in the center for 2 minutes each side. Transfer it to a prepared sheet. Pour any remaining oil from the skillet, wipe clean with a paper towel, and add the remaining 2 tablespoons olive oil.

4. On each tortilla, spread some avocado crema. Top with cabbage, a piece of fish, and a spoonful of mango salsa. Serve with lime wedges and extra crema and salsa on the side.

Nutrition Info:

- Per Serving: Calories: 523 ; Fat: 36g ;Protein: 12g ;Carbs: 46g .

Smoothies

Savoury Smoothie With Mango And Thyme

Servings: 1

Cooking Time: 0 Minutes

Ingredients:

- 1 cup fresh or frozen mango chunks
- ½ cup fresh green grapes, seedless
- ¼ fennel bulb
- ½ cup almond milk, unsweetened

- ½ teaspoon thyme leaves, fresh
- Pinch sea salt
- Pinch freshly ground black pepper
- Ice

Directions:

1. Combine in a blender the mango, grapes, fennel, almond milk, thyme leaves, sea salt, pepper, and ice. Blend until smooth.

Nutrition Info:

- Per Serving: Calories: 274 ;Fat: 4g ;Protein: 3g ;Carbs: 65g.

Minty Juice With Pineapple And Cucumber

Servings: 3 ½

Cooking Time: 0 Minutes

Ingredients:

- 1 large, ripe pineapple, skin removed and core intact
- ¼ cup mint leaves
- 1 cucumber

Directions:

1. Cut the pineapple in long strips that will fit through the juicer feed tube. Process the pineapple, adding the mint leaves in between pieces, on the proper setting of the juicer. Juice the cucumber, then stir. Serve immediately.

Nutrition Info:

- Per Serving: Calories: 9 ;Fat: 5g;Protein: 1g ;Carbs: 2g .

Handy Veggie Smoothie

Servings: 1

Cooking Time: 0 Minutes

Ingredients:

- 1 carrot, trimmed
- 1 small beet, scrubbed and quartered
- 1 celery stalk
- ½ cup raspberries, fresh

- 1 cup coconut water
- 1 teaspoon balsamic vinegar
- Ice

Directions:

1. In a blender, combine the carrot, beet, celery, raspberries, coconut water, balsamic vinegar, and ice and blend until smooth.

Nutrition Info:

- Per Serving: Calories: 140 ;Fat: 1g ;Protein: 3g ;Carbs: 24g.

Cheery Cherry Smoothie

Servings: 1
Cooking Time: 0 Minutes

Ingredients:

- 1 cup frozen pitted cherries, no-added-sugar
- ¼ cup fresh, or frozen, raspberries
- ¾ cup coconut water
- 1 tablespoon raw honey or maple syrup
- 1 teaspoon chia seeds
- 1 teaspoon hemp seeds
- Drop vanilla extract
- Ice

Directions:

1. Combine in a blender the cherries, raspberries, coconut water, honey, chia seeds, hemp seeds, vanilla, and ice. Blend until smooth.

Nutrition Info:

- Per Serving: Calories: 266 ;Fat: 2g ;Protein: 3g ;Carbs: 52g.

For Advanced Green Juice

Servings: ½
Cooking Time: 0 Minutes

Ingredients:

- 3 cups spinach, 120g
- 1 Granny Smith apple
- 1 cucumber
- 1 fennel bulb
- One 1 inch piece fresh ginger
- One 1 inch piece fresh turmeric
- Freshly ground black pepper
- 1 lemon

Directions:

1. Wash all the fruits and vegetables and pat dry. Juice the spinach, apple, cucumber, fennel, ginger, turmeric, and a pinch of pepper according to your juicer's instructions. Squeeze in the lemon juice and stir. Serve immediately then garnish with another pinch of pepper.

Nutrition Info:

- Per Serving: Calories: 225 ;Fat: 2g ;Protein: 225g ;Carbs: 51g.

Salad-like Green Smoothie

Servings: 1
Cooking Time: 0 Minutes

Ingredients:

- ¾ to 1 cup water
- 1 cup spinach leaves, lightly packed
- 2 kale leaves, thoroughly washed
- 2 romaine lettuce leaves
- ½ avocado
- 1 pear, stemmed, cored, and chopped

Directions:

1. Combine the water, spinach, kale, romaine lettuce, avocado, and pear in a blender.
2. Blend until smooth and serve.

Nutrition Info:

- Per Serving: Calories: 180 ;Fat: 10g ;Protein: 4g ;Carbs: 23g .

Refreshing Green Iced Tea With Ginger

Servings: 1
Cooking Time: 0 Minutes

Ingredients:

- 2 cups concentrated green or matcha tea, served hot
- ¼ cup crystalized ginger, chopped into fine pieces
- 1 sprig fresh mint

Directions:

1. Get a glass container and mix the tea with the ginger and then cover and chill for as long as time permits.
2. Strain and pour into serving glasses over ice if preferred.
3. Garnish with a wedge of lemon and a sprig of fresh mint to serve.

Nutrition Info:

- Per Serving: Calories: 206 ;Fat: 5g ;Protein: 2g ;Carbs: 38g .

Great Watermelon Smoothie

Servings: 1
Cooking Time: 0 Minutes

Ingredients:

- 1 cup watermelon chunks
- 2 cups mixed berries, frozen
- 1 cup coconut water
- 2 tablespoons chia seeds
- ½ cup tart cherries

Directions:

1. Blend ingredients in a blender or juicer until puréed.
2. Serve immediately and enjoy.

Nutrition Info:

- Per Serving: Calories: 1134 ;Fat: 26g ;Protein: 16g ;Carbs: 218g.

Smoothie That Can Soothe Inflammation

Servings: 1
Cooking Time: 0 Minutes

Ingredients:

- 1 pear, cored and quartered
- ½ fennel bulb
- 1 thin slice ginger, fresh
- 1 cup packed spinach
- ½ cucumber, peeled if wax-coated or not organic
- ½ cup water
- Ice

Directions:

1. Combine the pear, fennel, ginger, spinach, cucumber, water, and ice in a blender. Blend until smooth.

Nutrition Info:

- Per Serving: Calories: 147 ;Fat: 1g ;Protein: 4g ;Carbs: 37g .

Fabolous Minty Green Smoothie

Servings: 2
Cooking Time: 0 Minutes

Ingredients:

- 1 cup canned lite coconut milk
- 1 cup fresh spinach
- 1 banana, cut into chunks
- ½ avocado
- ½ English cucumber, cut into chunks
- 2 tablespoons fresh mint, chopped
- 1 tablespoon lemon juice, freshly squeezed
- 1 tablespoon raw honey
- 3 ice cubes

Directions:

1. Combine the coconut milk, spinach, banana, avocado, cucumber, mint, lemon juice, and honey in a blender. Blend until smooth.
2. Add the ice and blend until thick.

Nutrition Info:

- Per Serving: Calories: 482 ;Fat: 40g ;Protein: 6g;Carbs: 37g.

Pain Reliever Smoothie

Servings: 1
Cooking Time: 0 Minutes

Ingredients:

- 1 stalk celery, chopped
- 1 cup cucumber, chopped
- ½ cup pineapple, chopped
- ½ lemon, zest juice
- 1 cup coconut water
- 1 apple, chopped

Directions:

1. Take all of the ingredients except the lemon zest and blend until smooth.
2. You can add ice cubes at this point if you want it chilled.
3. Serve with a sprinkling of lemon zest.

Nutrition Info:

- Per Serving: Calories: 237 ;Fat: 1g ;Protein: 4g ;Carbs: 58g .

Tropical And Extra Red Smoothie

Servings: 2
Cooking Time: 0 Minutes

Ingredients:

- 1 cup coconut water
- ½ cup pineapple juice, unsweetened
- 1 banana
- ½ cup fresh raspberries
- ½ cup shredded coconut, unsweetened
- 3 ice cubes

Directions:

1. Combine the coconut water, pineapple juice, banana, raspberries, and coconut in a blender. Blend until smooth.
2. Add the ice and blend until thick.

Nutrition Info:

- Per Serving: Calories: 209 ;Fat: 10g ;Protein: 3g;Carbs: 31g .

Mediterranean Green On Green Smoothie

Servings: 1
Cooking Time: 0 Minutes

Ingredients:

- 1 cup packed baby spinach
- ½ green apple
- 1 tablespoon maple syrup
- ¼ teaspoon cinnamon, ground
- 1 cup almond milk, unsweetened
- ½ cup ice

Directions:

1. Combine all the ingredients in a blender and blend until smooth. Serve.

Nutrition Info:

- Per Serving: Calories: 130 ;Fat: 4g ;Protein: 2g ;Carbs: 23g .

Fantastic Fruity Smoothie

Servings: 1
Cooking Time: 0 Minutes

Ingredients:

- 2 cups carrots, peeled and sliced
- 2 cups filtered water
- 1 apple, peeled and sliced
- 1 banana, peeled and sliced
- 1 cup fresh pineapple, peeled and sliced
- ½ tablespoon ginger, grated
- ¼ teaspoon turmeric, ground
- 1 tablespoon lemon juice
- 1 cup almond or soy milk

Directions:

1. Blend carrots and water to make a puréed carrot juice.
2. Pour into a Mason jar or sealable container, cover and place in the fridge.
3. Add the rest of the smoothie ingredients once done to a blender or juicer until smooth.
4. Add the carrot juice in at the end, blending thoroughly until smooth.
5. Serve with or without ice.

Nutrition Info:

- Per Serving: Calories: 367 ;Fat: 5g ;Protein: 6g ;Carbs: 80g.

Wild Blueberry Smoothie With Chocolate And Turmeric

Servings: 2
Cooking Time: 0 Minutes

Ingredients:

- 2 cups almond milk, unsweetened
- 1 cup wild blueberries, frozen
- 2 tablespoons cocoa powder
- 1 to 2 packets stevia, or to taste
- One 1 inch piece fresh turmeric, peeled
- 1 cup ice, crushed

Directions:

1. Combine in a blender the almond milk, blueberries, cocoa powder, stevia, turmeric, and ice. Blend until smooth.

Nutrition Info:

- Per Serving: Calories: 97 ;Fat: 5g ;Protein: 3g ;Carbs: 16g .

Popular Banana Smoothie With Kale

Servings: 2

Cooking Time: 0 Minutes

Ingredients:

- 2 cups almond milk, unsweetened
- 2 cups kale, stemmed, leaves chopped
- 2 bananas, peeled
- 1 to 2 packets stevia, or to taste
- 1 teaspoon cinnamon, ground
- 1 cup ice, crushed

Directions:

1. Combine the almond milk, kale, bananas, stevia, cinnamon, and ice in a blender. Blend until smooth.

Nutrition Info:

- Per Serving: Calories: 181 ;Fat: 4g ;Protein: 4g ;Carbs: 37g .

Desserts

Peanut Chocolate Brownies

Servings: 6
Cooking Time: 40 Minutes

Ingredients:

- 1 ¾ cups whole-grain flour
- 1 tsp baking powder
- ½ tsp sea salt
- 1 tbsp ground nutmeg
- ½ tsp ground cinnamon
- 3 tbsp cocoa powder
- ½ cup dark chocolate chips
- ½ cup chopped peanuts
- ¼ cup canola oil
- ½ cup dark molasses
- 3 tbsp pure date sugar
- 2 tsp grated fresh ginger

Directions:

1. Preheat your oven to 360ºF. Combine the flour, baking powder, salt, nutmeg, cinnamon, and cocoa in a bowl. Add in chocolate chips and peanuts and stir. Set aside. In another bowl, mix the oil, molasses, ½ cup water, date sugar, and ginger. Pour into the flour mixture and stir to combine. Transfer to a greased baking pan and bake for 30-35 minutes. Let cool before slicing.

Nutrition Info:

- Per Serving: Calories: 430;Fat: 19g;Protein: 12g;Carbs: 58g.

Mini Chocolate Fudge Squares

Servings: 6
Cooking Time: 20 Minutes + Chilling Time

Ingredients:

- 2 cups coconut cream
- 1 tsp vanilla extract
- 3 oz almond butter
- 3 oz dark chocolate

Directions:

1. Pour coconut cream and vanilla into a saucepan and bring to a boil over medium heat, then simmer until reduced by half, 15 minutes. Stir in almond butter until the batter is smooth. Chop the dark chocolate into bits and stir in the cream until melted. Pour the mixture into a round baking sheet. Chill in the fridge for 3 hours. Serve sliced.

Nutrition Info:

- Per Serving: Calories: 445;Fat: 44g;Protein: 4g;Carbs: 14g.

Tasty Haystack Cookies From Missouri

Servings: 24
Cooking Time: 1 ½ Hours

Ingredients:

- ½ cup coconut oil
- ½ cup almond milk, unsweetened
- 1 overripe banana, mashed well
- ½ cup coconut sugar
- ¼ cup cacao powder
- 1 teaspoon vanilla extract
- ¼ teaspoon sea salt
- 3 cups rolled oats
- ½ cup almond butter

Directions:

1. Stir together in a medium bowl the coconut oil, almond milk, mashed banana, coconut sugar, cacao powder, vanilla, and salt. Pour the mixture into the slow cooker.
2. Pour the oats on top without stirring.
3. Put the almond butter on top of the oats without stirring.
4. Cover the cooker and set to high. Cook for 1½ hours.
5. Stir the mixture well. Scoop tablespoon-size balls out as it cools and press onto a baking sheet to continue to cool. Serve when hardened. Keep leftovers refrigerated in an airtight container for up to 1 week.

Nutrition Info:

- Per Serving: Calories: 140 ;Fat: 9g ;Protein: 2g ;Carbs: 14g .

Coconut & Chocolate Cake

Servings: 4
Cooking Time: 40 Minutes + Cooling Time

Ingredients:

- 2/3 cup almond flour
- ¼ cup almond butter, melted
- 2 cups chocolate bars, cubed
- 2 ½ cups coconut cream
- Fresh berries for topping

Directions:

1. Mix the almond flour and almond butter in a medium bowl and pour the mixture into a greased springform pan. Use the spoon to spread and press the mixture into the pan. Place in the refrigerator to firm for 30 minutes.
2. Meanwhile, pour the chocolate in a safe microwave bowl and melt for 1 minute stirring every 30 seconds. Remove from the microwave and mix in the coconut cream and maple syrup. Remove the cake pan from the oven, pour the chocolate mixture on top, and shake the pan and even the layer. Chill further for 4 to 6 hours. Take out the pan from the fridge, release the cake and garnish with the raspberries or strawberries. Slice and serve.

Nutrition Info:

- Per Serving: Calories: 985;Fat: 62g;Protein: 9g;Carbs: 108g.

Spiced Supreme Orange

Servings: 2
Cooking Time: 15 Minutes

Ingredients:

- ½ cup water
- 1 tablespoon raw honey
- 1 lemon
- 1 small cinnamon stick
- 1 clove
- 2 oranges, peeled and sectioned
- 1 sprig fresh mint

Directions:

1. Add all of the ingredients except the oranges to a saucepan.
2. Cook over a medium heat until thickened for 10 to 15 minutes.
3. Add the oranges, and then simmer for a minute.
4. Transfer all ingredients to a bowl or container and place in the fridge, marinate for 2 hours or preferably overnight.
5. Drain orange slices and garnish with a little fresher mint to serve.
6. Best served with low fat Greek yogurt for summer or warmed through in the winter.

Nutrition Info:

- Per Serving: Calories: 128 ;Fat: 3g ;Protein: 12g;Carbs: 27g .

Mango & Coconut Rice Pudding

Servings: 4
Cooking Time: 25 Minutes

Ingredients:

- 1 can coconut milk
- 1 mango, sliced
- ¼ cup caster sugar
- 1 tsp ground ginger
- A pinch of sea salt
- 2 cups cooked brown rice

Directions:

1. Place the sugar, ginger, and salt in a pot over medium heat and cook for 3-4 minutes until the sugar dissolves. Mix in brown rice and cook for another 3 minutes until the rice is heated through. Spoon into serving bowls and top with the sliced mango. Serve and enjoy!

Nutrition Info:

- Per Serving: Calories: 626;Fat: 21g;Protein: 9.4g;Carbs: 99g.

Chocolate Campanelle With Hazelnuts

Servings: 4
Cooking Time: 10 Minutes

Ingredients:

- ½ cup chopped toasted hazelnuts
- ¼ cup dark chocolate chips
- 8 oz campanelle pasta
- 3 tbsp almond butter
- ¼ cup maple syrup

Directions:

1. Pulse the hazelnuts and chocolate pieces in a food processor until crumbly. Set aside. Place the campanelle pasta in a pot with boiling salted water. Cook for 8-10 minutes until al dente, stirring often. Drain and back to the pot. Stir in almond butter and maple syrup and stir until the butter is melted. Serve garnished with chocolate-hazelnut mixture.

Nutrition Info:

- Per Serving: Calories: 360;Fat: 20g;Protein: 4g;Carbs: 44g.

Lemon Blackberry Cake

Servings: 4
Cooking Time: 45 Minutes

Ingredients:

- 4 peeled peaches, sliced
- 2 cups fresh blackberries
- 1 tbsp arrowroot
- ¾ cup pure date sugar
- 2 tsp fresh lemon juice
- 1 tsp ground cinnamon
- ½ cup whole-grain flour
- ½ cup old-fashioned oats
- 3 tbsp almond butter

Directions:

1. Preheat your oven to 370ºF. In a bowl, mix the peaches, blackberries, arrowroot, ¼ cup of sugar, lemon juice, and ½ tsp of cinnamon. Pour the batter into the pan. Set aside. In a bowl, stir the flour, oats, almond butter, remaining cup of sugar, and remaining cinnamon. Blend until crumbly. Drizzle the topping over the fruit. Bake for 30-40 minutes until browned. Serve.

Nutrition Info:

- Per Serving: Calories: 370;Fat: 10g;Protein: 6g;Carbs: 73g.

Vanilla Berry Tarts

Servings: 4
Cooking Time: 35 Minutes + Cooling Time

Ingredients:

- 4 eggs, beaten
- 1/3 cup whole-wheat flour
- ½ tsp salt
- ¼ cup almond butter
- 3 tbsp pure malt syrup
- 6 oz coconut cream
- 6 tbsp pure date sugar
- ¾ tsp vanilla extract
- 1 cup mixed frozen berries

Directions:

1. Preheat your oven to 350ºF. In a large bowl, combine flour and salt. Add almond butter and whisk until crumbly. Pour in the eggs and malt syrup and mix until smooth dough forms. Flatten the dough on a flat surface, cover with plastic wrap, and refrigerate for 1 hour.

2. Dust a working surface with some flour, remove the dough onto the surface, and using a rolling pin, flatten the dough into a 1-inch diameter circle. Use a large cookie cutter, cut out rounds of the dough and fit into the pie pans. Use a knife to trim the edges of the pan. Lay a parchment paper on the dough cups, pour on some baking beans, and bake in the oven until golden brown, 15-20 minutes. Remove the pans from the oven, pour out the baking beans, and allow cooling. In a bowl, mix coconut cream, date sugar, and vanilla extract. Divide the mixture into the tart cups and top with berries. Serve.

Nutrition Info:

- Per Serving: Calories: 590;Fat: 38g;Protein: 13g;Carbs: 56g.

Poached Pears With Green Tea

Servings: 4
Cooking Time: 15 Minutes

Ingredients:

- 4 pears, peeled, cored, and quartered lengthwise
- 2 cups green tea, strongly brewed
- ¼ cup honey
- 1 tablespoon fresh ginger, grated

Directions:

1. Combine the pears, tea, honey, and ginger in a large pot over medium-high heat. Bring to a simmer. Lower the heat to medium-low, cover, and simmer for 15 minutes until the pears soften. Serve the pears with the poaching liquid spooned over the top.

Nutrition Info:

- Per Serving: Calories: 190 ;Fat: 6g;Protein: 23g;Carbs: 50g .

Tropical Cheesecake

Servings: 4
Cooking Time: 20 Minutes + Cooling Time

Ingredients:

- 2/3 cup toasted rolled oats
- ¼ cup almond butter, melted
- 3 tbsp pure date sugar
- 6 oz coconut cream
- ¼ cup coconut milk
- 1 lemon, zested and juiced
- 3 tsp agar agar powder
- 1 ripe mango, chopped

Directions:

1. Process the oats, almond butter, and date sugar in a blender until smooth. Pour the mixture into a greased springform pan and press the mixture onto the bottom of the pan. Refrigerate for 30 minutes until firm while you make the filling. In a large bowl, using an electric mixer, whisk the coconut cream until smooth. Beat in coconut milk, lemon zest, and lemon juice.

2. Mix ¼ cup of hot water and agar agar powder until dissolved and whisk this mixture into the creamy mix. Fold in mango. Remove the cake pan from the fridge and pour in the mango mixture. Shake the pan to ensure smooth layering on top. Refrigerate for at least 3 hours.

Nutrition Info:

- Per Serving: Calories: 315;Fat: 28g;Protein: 5g;Carbs: 15g.

Full Coconut Cake

Servings: 4
Cooking Time: 55 Minutes

Ingredients:

- 3 eggs, yolks and whites separated
- ¾ cup coconut flour
- ½ tsp coconut extract
- 1 ½ cups coconut milk
- ½ cup coconut sugar
- 2 tbsp melted coconut oil

Directions:

1. Beat the whites until soft form peaks. Beat in the egg yolks along with the coconut sugar. Stir in coconut extract and coconut oil. Gently fold in the coconut flour. Line a baking dish and pour the batter inside. Cover with aluminum foil. Pour 1 cup of water into your Instant Pot. Place the dish in the pressure cooker. Seal the lid and cook for 45 minutes on "Manual". Serve and enjoy.

Nutrition Info:

- Per Serving: Calories: 350;Fat: 14g;Protein: 8g;Carbs: 47g.

Nutty Date Cake

Servings: 4
Cooking Time:1 Hour 30 Minutes

Ingredients:

- ½ cup cold almond butter, cut into pieces
- 1 egg, beaten
- ½ cup whole-wheat flour
- ¼ cup chopped nuts
- 1 tsp baking powder
- 1 tsp baking soda
- 1 tsp cinnamon powder
- 1 tsp salt
- 1/3 cup dates, chopped
- ½ cup pure date sugar
- 1 tsp vanilla extract
- ¼ cup pure date syrup

Directions:

1. Preheat your oven to 350ºF. In a food processor, add the flour, nuts, baking powder, baking soda, cinnamon powder, and salt. Blend until well combined. Add 1/3 cup of water, almond butter, dates, date sugar, and vanilla. Process until smooth with tiny pieces of dates evident.

2. Pour the batter into a greased baking dish. Bake in the oven for 1 hour and 10 minutes or until a toothpick inserted comes out clean. Remove the dish from the oven, invert the cake onto a serving platter to cool, drizzle with the date syrup, slice, and serve.

Nutrition Info:

- Per Serving: Calories: 440;Fat: 28g;Protein: 8g;Carbs: 48g.

Mango Chocolate Fudge

Servings: 3
Cooking Time: 10 Minutes + Chilling Time

Ingredients:

- 1 mango, pureed
- ¾ cup dark chocolate chips
- 4 cups pure date sugar

Directions:

1. Microwave the chocolate until melted. Add in the pureed mango and date sugar and stir to combine. Spread on a lined with waxed paper baking pan and chill in the fridge for 2 hours. Take out the fudge and lay on a cutting board. Slice into small pieces and serve.

Nutrition Info:

- Per Serving: Calories: 730;Fat: 1g;Protein: 2g;Carbs: 182g.

Coconut & Chocolate Brownies

Servings: 4
Cooking Time: 40 Minutes

Ingredients:

- 1 cup whole-grain flour
- ½ cup cocoa powder
- 1 tsp baking powder
- ½ tsp salt
- 1 cup pure date sugar
- ½ cup canola oil
- ¾ cup almond milk
- 1 tsp pure vanilla extract
- 1 tsp coconut extract
- ½ cup dark chocolate chips
- ½ cup shredded coconut

Directions:

1. Preheat your oven to 360ºF. In a bowl, combine the flour, cocoa, baking powder, and salt. In another bowl, whisk the date sugar and oil until creamy. Add in almond milk, vanilla, and coconut. Mix until smooth. Pour into the flour mixture and stir to combine. Fold in the coconut and chocolate chips. Pour the batter into a greased baking pan and bake for 35-40 minutes. Serve chilled.

Nutrition Info:

- Per Serving: Calories: 600;Fat: 31g;Protein: 7g;Carbs: 83g.

Vanilla Brownies

Servings: 4
Cooking Time: 30 Minutes + Chilling Time

Ingredients:

- 2 eggs
- ¼ cup cocoa powder
- ½ cup almond flour
- ½ tsp baking powder
- ½ cup stevia
- 10 tbsp almond butter
- 2 oz dark chocolate
- ½ tsp vanilla extract

Directions:

1. Preheat your oven to 375ºF. In a bowl, mix cocoa powder, almond flour, baking powder, and stevia until no lumps. In another bowl, add the almond butter and dark chocolate and melt both in the microwave for 30 seconds to 1 minute.

2. Whisk the eggs and vanilla into the chocolate mixture, then pour the mixture into the dry ingredients. Combine evenly. Pour the batter onto a paper-lined baking sheet and bake for 20 minutes. Cool completely and refrigerate for 2 hours. When ready, slice into squares and serve.

Nutrition Info:

- Per Serving: Calories: 300;Fat: 32g;Protein: 3g;Carbs: 6g.

Appendix:Recipes Index

A

African Zucchini Salad 24

All Green Salad With Basil-cherry Dressing 22

Almond & Raisin Granola 10

Almond Flour English Muffins 6

Appealing Lemon With Wild Salmon And Mixed Vegetables 53

Appetizing And Healthy Turkey Gumbo 45

Appetizing Casserole With Broccoli And Bean 27

Apple-glazed Whole Chicken 44

Arugula Salad With Salmon 19

B

Blueberry Smoothie With Ginger 9

Breakfast Bake Millet With Blueberry 5

Breakfast Vanilla Quinoa Bowl 8

Broccoli Hash Browns 5

Brussels Sprouts & Tofu Soup 39

C

Caramelized Roasted Fennel With Sunflower Seed Pesto 14

Carrot Salad With Cherries & Pecans 22

Carrot-strawberry Smoothie 10

Cayenne Pumpkin Soup 39

Cheery Cherry Smoothie 59

Cheesy Cauliflower Casserole 33

Chicken & Ginger Soup 35

Chicken Stir-fry With Bell Pepper 42

Chinese Fried Rice 30

Choco-berry Smoothie 10

Chocolate Campanelle With Hazelnuts 66

Coconut & Chocolate Brownies 70

Coconut & Chocolate Cake 65

Cold Vegetable Soup 37

Commercial And Mild Curry Powder 14

Convenient Salad With Raspberry Vinaigrette, Spinach, And Walnut 21

Creamy Crabmeat 57

Creamy Dressing With Sesame 12

Crispy Pan-seared Salmon 51

Cucumber & Pear Rice Salad 22

Cumin Lamb Meatballs With Aioli 47

D

Dairy Free Apple Cider Vinegar With Tangy Barbecue Sauce 15

Dazzling And Smoky Salmon Hash Browns 56

Decadent And Simple Alfredo With Cauliflower 17

Delicious Pesto With Kale 15

F

Fabolous Minty Green Smoothie 61

Fantastic Fruity Smoothie 62

Favourite Pizza With Quinoa Flatbread 28

For Advanced Green Juice 59

Fragrant Coconut Fruit Salad 20

Fragrant Peach Butter 13

Fresh Maple Dressing 18

Full Coconut Cake 68

G

Game Changer Pickled Red Onions 16

Garlicky Sauce With Tahini 13

Gingered Beef Stir-fry With Peppers 45

Great Watermelon Smoothie 60

Greatest Crispy Fish Tacos And Mango Salsa 57

Green Bean & Rice Soup 38

Green Bean & Zucchini Velouté 37

Green Veggie Frittata 7

Grilled Adobo Shrimp Skewers 51

H

Habanero Pinto Bean & Bell Pepper Pot 26

Handy Veggie Smoothie 58

Hawaiian Tuna 50

Hazelnut Crusted Trout Fillets 52

Herby Green Whole Chicken 43

Homemade Burgers With Bean And Yam 26

Homemade Chicken & Pepper Cacciatore 48

I

Italian Turkey Meatballs 44

K

Korean Vegetable Salad With Smoky Crispy Kalua Pork 49

L

Lemon & Caper Turkey Scaloppine 43

Lemon Blackberry Cake 67

Lime Salmon Burgers 54

M

Magical One-pot Tomato Basil Pasta 32

Magnificent Herbaceous Pork Meatballs 42

Mango & Coconut Rice Pudding 66

Mango Chocolate Fudge 69

Mango Rice Pudding 6

Mango Rice Salad With Lime Dressing 21

Mediterranean Green On Green Smoothie 62

Mediterranean Stew With Lentil And Broccoli 41

Mini Chocolate Fudge Squares 64

Minty Eggplant Salad 21

Minty Juice With Pineapple And Cucumber 58

Morning Matcha & Ginger Shake 8

N

Native Asian Soup With Squash And Shitake 34

Natural Dressing With Ginger And Turmeric 18

No-bread Avocado Sandwich 11

Nostalgic Tuna And Avocado Salad Sandwiches 55

Nut Free Turkey Burgers With Ginger 46

Nutritious Bowl With Lentil, Vegetable, And Fruit 25

Nutty Date Cake 69

O

Old Bay Crab Cakes 54

Old Fashioned Dressing With Lemon And Mustard 12

Omelette With Smoky Shrimp 9

One-pot Chunky Beef Stew 34

Orange-carrot Muffins With Cherries 7

Out Of This World Salad With Basil And Tomato 23

P

Pain Reliever Smoothie 61

Peanut Chocolate Brownies 64

Peanuty Sugar Snaps With Lime And Satay Tofu 30

Poached Pears With Green Tea 68

Popular Banana Smoothie With Kale 63

Power Green Soup 40

Pressure Cooked Ratatouille 27

Refreshing Green Iced Tea With Ginger 60

Rice Noodle Soup With Beans 37

Rosemary White Bean Soup 36

S

Salad-like Green Smoothie 59

Salmon In Miso-ginger Sauce 56

Satisfying And Thick Dressing With Avocado 17

Savoury Smoothie With Mango And Thyme 58

Seitan Cauliflower Gratin 31

Smoky Boneless Haddock With Pea Risotto 55

Smoothie That Can Soothe Inflammation 60

Soft Zucchini With White Beans And Olives Stuffing 28

Soulful Roasted Vegetable Soup 36

Spiced Supreme Orange 66

Spicy And Tasty Indian Cauliflower And Broccoli Rabe 32

Spicy Shrimp Scampi 53

Spinach & Pomegranate Salad 19

Spinach Salad With Cranberries 23

Strawberry & Pecan Breakfast 6

Summer Salad 24

Summer Time Sizzling Green Salad With Salmon 20

Superb Salad With Chickpea 23

Sweet Balsamic Chicken 49

T

Tasty Haystack Cookies From Missouri 65

Tasty Sardine Donburi 52

Tastylicious Chicken Cajun With Prawn 48

Teriyaki Vegetable Stir-fry 27

To Die For Homemade Mayonnaise 16

Tofu Scramble 8

Traditional And Delightful Gremolata Sauce 16

Traditional Beef Bolognese 46

Traditional Cilantro Pilaf 29

Tricky Cheesy Yellow Sauce 17

Tropical And Extra Red Smoothie 61

Tropical Cheesecake 68

Turmeric Cauliflower Soup 38

V

Vanilla Berry Tarts 67

Vanilla Brownies 70

Vegetable & Hummus Pizza 29

Vegetable Chili 40

Veggie & Beef Brisket 47

W

Watercress & Mushroom Spaghetti 31

Wild Blueberry Smoothie With Chocolate And Turmeric 62

Winterrific Soup With Chicken And Dumpling 35

Wonderful Baked Sea Bass With Tomatoes, Olives, And Capers 50

Printed in Great Britain
by Amazon

28669436R00048